CONVICTIONS OF
THE HEART

A gift from AFSC to the
Davis Friends Meeting
December, 1989

Convictions of the Heart

\(1973-\)

JIM CORBETT AND
THE SANCTUARY MOVEMENT

Miriam Davidson

THE UNIVERSITY OF ARIZONA PRESS, TUCSON

THE UNIVERSITY OF ARIZONA PRESS

Copyright © 1988
The Arizona Board of Regents
All Rights Reserved

This book was set in 10/12 Linotron 202 Sabon.
Manufactured in the United States of America

Library of Congress Cataloging-in-Publication Data

Davidson, Miriam.
Convictions of the heart.

Bibliography: p.
Includes index.
1. Sanctuary movement.   2. Church work with
refugees—United States.   3. Refugees, Political—
Central America.   4. Corbett, Jim, 1933–
I. Title.
HV645.D38   1988   261.8'32   88-4796
Cloth ISBN 0-8165-1034-2 (alk. paper)
Paper ISBN 0-8165-1107-1 (alk. paper)

Second printing 1988

British Library Cataloguing in Publication data are available.

To David

CONTENTS

ILLUSTRATIONS

CONVICTIONS OF
THE HEART

THE INNER LIGHT

The year was 1742, and young John Woolman, a Quaker from the New Jersey countryside, had a new job as an assistant to a shopkeeper in nearby Mount Holly. Woolman had been at the shop for only a few months when, to his surprise and dismay, his boss asked him to write out a bill of sale for a slave. Woolman's religion taught that it was against God's law to hold humans in oppression—that all people were equal before God—and he believed this so strongly that he said so at the time. But as he was a mere employee, and the man buying the slave was an esteemed member of the local Religious Society of Friends, or Quakers, Woolman acquiesced and wrote out the bill of sale.

He at once regretted it, and the incident weighed heavily on his mind. Less than a year later it influenced his decision to begin what would become his life's vocation: touring the colonies, speaking against slavery to Quakers and Quaker meetings, and writing anti-slavery articles (some of which were published by his friend Benjamin Franklin). Woolman also dedicated himself to living a life free of the fruits of slavery. When he visited slave-holding Friends, he insisted on paying for his food and lodging. At home in Mount Holly, he gave up being a merchant, for it was making him rich, and Woolman could not escape his conviction that some people were rich because most people were poor. He took up tailoring instead, and in his new occupation he refused to use the fashionable indigo-dyed cloth that was made from the torturous labor of slaves. More than thirty years before the United States became a nation, more than a hundred years before the Civil War, Woolman wrote, "The seeds of great calamity and desolation are sown and growing fast on this continent." Seeing what was ahead, the Quaker pledged, in his own life, to do something about it.

Among Friends, he was largely successful. By the end of the eighteenth century, only a few Quakers in the South still held slaves. Woolman, and those who followed him, appealed to the consciences of slave-holding Friends by asking them to follow their "Inner Light" —the Quaker version of Jiminy Cricket's "Let your conscience be your guide." Woolman didn't preach self-righteously. He believed that, if each person asked humbly for the truth, it would be revealed to him.

But society as a whole ignored the message of John Woolman. The abolitionists, who believed slave owners should be forced to give up their slaves, gained power. In an ironic twist of history, by the 1830s the Quakers, who were among the first American religions to renounce slavery, had to withdraw from a leadership role in the anti-slavery cause. Friends were as committed to nonviolence as they were to freeing the slaves, and they refused to countenance the coercive, and sometimes violent, methods advocated by abolitionist leaders. Some well-known Quakers, such as Levi Coffin and Thomas Garrett, continued to shelter runaway slaves on the underground railroad, but other Friends who publicly supported the abolitionists were "read out" of their Meetings. Quakers were soon branded as "gradualists," traitors, and worse in abolitionist newspapers.

A bloody war and a century of struggle later, our nation still carried the scars of the evil system of slavery. Perhaps it can be said that the Quaker way failed, or perhaps no one ever gave it a chance to work. But in a world where people are all too ready to force others to conform to their version of truth, we would do well to heed the words of British author G. M. Trevelyan: "Close your ears to John Woolman one century, and you will get John Brown the next, with Grant to follow."

Two hundred and forty years later, on the other side of the continent, another American Quaker had an experience similar to Woolman's writing of the bill of sale. Like his predecessor, Jim Corbett was led to become concerned about justice and liberty for human beings whom many Americans considered less than equal. This book tells the story of his attempt to bring the truth of their suffering to light. In part because of modern communications, Corbett's quixotic quest had a greater immediate effect than Woolman's. Whether, ultimately, his message will go the way of Woolman's is up to us.

A Quiet
Testimony

The first burning fingers of light reached over the mountaintops, illuminating a scene of horror on the desert floor below. Twenty-one human shapes, naked, dirty, and covered with cactus thorns, lay among their scattered belongings. Their lips were dried and cracked, their skin red and swollen. Some of these half-dead beings tried to escape the sunrise by dragging their bodies into shadow, but the searing white light crushed their will to live as rapidly as it filled the eastern sky. The Salvadorans knew that, without water, this would be their last day on earth.

Two nights earlier, this group of mostly middle-class city-dwellers had entered the United States. They had left behind family, friends, and familiar surroundings and trustingly followed two Mexican guides—a father and son—through a barbed-wire fence, over a mountain range, and halfway across the wide valley where they now lay. The guides (called coyotes) assured them the walk would be short, ten miles at most, and so no one bothered to conserve what little water they had brought. It ran out the first morning.

Early in their first day in the desert, the father-coyote disappeared. Two young men, both students at the University of San Salvador, went with him. About midday, the other Mexican coyote left, saying he was going to get water, and a stocky housewife named Berta got to her feet and insisted that she go, too. They were supposed to have been back in a couple hours. Neither had been seen since. The Salvadorans who stayed overcame their disgust and began to save and drink their urine.

None had any idea how to protect themselves from the 120-degree temperatures. Thinking it would help, the men and all but the most modest women took off their clothes. In the late afternoon, a middle-aged woman they had nicknamed La Gorda—the Fat Lady —succumbed to the heat with a violent shudder.

Evening fell, and two of the younger women felt well enough to brave the desert. The others moved a little ways away from the corpse of La Gorda, lit a fire, and waited for the coyotes to return.

Now, with the dawning of the second day, the Salvadorans realized that the coyotes were not coming back. Some of the men decided they had to go look for water themselves. They had no idea where they were, and they could see no signs of civilization—only jagged mountains rising from a dry sea. The sun was baking the earth. The desert shimmered in the glare. Slowly, the men got to their feet and began to stagger toward the east, where they remembered the young coyote had gone. Even the religious old man they respectfully called "Don" Cruz wanted to go. The women begged him not to, but he took his Bible and urine jug and crawled off. He soon lagged far behind the other men, and they had to leave him. Don Cruz was not seen again.

One man stayed with the women. Carlos Rivera, the 26-year-old Salvadoran coyote who had arranged this trip, felt no obligation to look for water. He preferred to watch the young women in their bras and panties. Rivera lay propped against a palo verde tree, belly hanging over his trousers and long, greasy hair tangled around his face. His presence made the women nervous.

They had reason to dislike him. In San Salvador, Rivera had taken $1,200 apiece for what he'd promised would be a plane trip into Los Angeles. His newspaper advertisement had said all border crossings were arranged, and many of the people on the bus believed it. Some of the others knew better, having been on Rivera's single, previous—and unsuccessful—attempt to bring a group into the United States. But they felt they had no alternative. In El Salvador during the first half of 1980, a coyote could promise anything and charge any amount and still have more than enough customers. Rivera, who operated out of a television repair shop, had grossly overbooked this trip. When the bus left the capital city during the last week of June, there were some forty adults and at least a half-dozen small children on it.

They were a varied group: students, housewives, factory workers, a bus driver, and a shoemaker, among others. Most were strangers to one another, and they did not develop a great deal of camaraderie during the trip. Their country was on the verge of civil war. The government's violent refusal to allow even minimal improvement in the lives of peasants and workers had polarized El Salvador into extremes of right and left. Official lawlessness had generated a climate of such fear that no one dared discuss personal business with anyone. During the 1960s, the government had organized a civilian paramilitary group, known by its acronym, ORDEN, to spy on people and report suspicious activity. In recent years, ORDEN members and soldiers in civilian clothes had become active, roaming the streets at night, taking people from their beds and leaving their tortured bodies for their families to find in the morning. The Archbishop of San Salvador, Arturo Rivera y Damas, estimated in June that 2,056 people, not including members of the security forces or the guerrillas, had been killed by political violence during the first five months of 1980. Few people in El Salvador, which at that time had a population of five million, were untouched by the carnage.

One young man on the bus had a friend who failed to show up for a second tour of duty in the National Guard. ORDEN members came to his house one night and took him away. The next day, the boy's body was found in the dump. His teeth had been broken off at the gums and his lips sewn together. His fingers had been crushed by a truck. When his torturers were finished, they ran the truck slowly over his body to kill him. Another young man on the bus was a student who had witnessed a massacre in a classroom at the university. Another passenger, a tall, quiet woman in her thirties, was from the northern province of Chalatenango. A state of undeclared war there between government troops and leftist guerrillas had left many people without homes or livelihoods. Refugees were pouring into San Salvador. The vicar of the provincial diocese of Chalatenango had summed up the situation for his church workers this way: "The people have three choices. They can join the left and be killed by the right. They can join the right and be killed by the left. Or they can leave the country."

Not everyone on this trip was fleeing political violence. Some were coming to America to join their spouses or to escape the factory shutdowns, strikes, and general economic paralysis in San Salvador. Coyotes like Carlos Rivera didn't care why their passengers wanted to go to the States; those who were fleeing for their lives and those leaving to get better jobs all had to pay the same price and take the same chances.

The four-day trip through Guatemala and Mexico was arduous but uneventful. When they reached the U.S. border, Rivera split up the group, sending the women with young children through Yuma, where he had tried and failed to sneak fifteen people into the United States two months before. It was easier to make the crossing there, but it was also riskier, as the U.S. Border Patrol tended to focus on populated areas. Rivera didn't want to chance having his entire group arrested, and he took everyone else on the bus back to Sonoyta, a tiny Mexican town about 120 miles east of Yuma. Sonoyta lay directly across the border from the Organ Pipe Cactus National Monument. Rivera assumed—rightly, it turned out—that the U.S. Border Patrol would not be expecting anyone to cross an uninhabited stretch of Sonoran Desert in the dead of summer.

Organ Pipe National Monument occupied 516 square miles on the southwest border of Arizona. Almost no rain fell there, but rather than being an empty wasteland, the park was home to a variety of plants and animals well-adapted to the hostile climate. Some were unique to the Sonoran desert; according to the Park Service guidebook, Organ Pipe National Monument was the only place in the United States where organ pipe cacti grew. Organ pipes are cousins of giant saguaros, the tall, long-armed cacti that range all over southwestern Arizona and northern Sonora, Mexico. The stunted and scraggly mesquite and palo verde trees offered little shade, but they were among the few objects in the landscape the Salvadorans could crawl under. Cholla cacti, sometimes known as jumping chollas, sank fierce inch-long spines into anything foolish enough to come near. Teddy-bear chollas, so named because their dense white thorns look soft and fuzzy, always claimed a few victims. The Salvadorans didn't know to use a stick to fling the cholla-branches away. They tried to pull them out, which only made the spines dig deep into their hands.

In a Sonoyta restaurant, Rivera hooked up with a smuggling ring called Los Muñecos—the Dolls. He needed help bringing his group through unfamiliar territory, and he sat at the bar with the leader of the Dolls, making plans. Many of the male Salvadorans, on the threshold of their dream, were drinking heavily that night. The women, disapproving, abstained. After several beers, the Doll-boss began propositioning the prettiest Salvadoran girls. "You can cross as my wife, in my car," he said. "I have a green card for you." The girls rejected his offers, and that made the Doll-boss mad. Later, after hiking almost 30 miles into the desert, the father-coyote told the women that he'd been directed to take them that way as punishment. He admitted he didn't even know where he was.

Rivera was not entirely responsible for their troubles, but enough to make the women despise him. They also hated the way he leered at them, even now, with their skin sunburned and bloodied by cactus spines. Trying to ignore him, the women knelt in a circle and prayed.

Rivera had his eye on three girls in particular. They were sisters, aged 12, 14, and 19. Twelve-year-old Claudia Huezo was the youngest in the group. She and her sisters were traveling unchaperoned, because their mother, who worked as a maid in Los Angeles, was anxious to get them out of El Salvador before the situation there got any worse. An uncle had gone to the U.S. embassy in San Salvador and tried to arrange visas for them. Out of the question, he was told. So their mother turned to Rivera, who, for $3,600, promised to bring her girls in by airplane. Now, prayers over, he wiggled over to where the Huezo sisters were lying. He squeezed himself between them. They were too weak to protest.

Suddenly, a woman lying nearby went into spasms. It was the one they called Chalatenango, after her home province. Men had approached her during the trip, but she remained aloof, something the other women respected her for. Now they watched in horror as she turned bright red, then blue, then gray. Chalatenango was choking to death.

The coyotes had showed them the old desert trick of putting smooth stones in the mouth to help keep saliva flowing. Chalatenango had swallowed one of hers. Rivera crawled over and struck the woman in the back several times, a maneuver that probably caused the rock to lodge more firmly in her throat. Then he grabbed a small spoon. He jammed it down her throat so hard a spurt of blood gushed out. He had punctured her esophagus. Rivera kept scraping away, but in a few minutes, Chalatenango was dead.

Shocked, the other women reacted with a frantic effort to save themselves. They made patches of shade by draping clothes over a palo verde tree. A middle-aged housewife named Guadalupe tossed her red blouse on top of the tree, hoping to signal a passing plane. Another woman laid out her makeup mirror for the same reason. As a last resort, they placed Bibles and crucifixes among the branches.

Cosmetics, the women realized, would help protect their skin from the sun. Rivera liked the idea. He let the women make him up in foundation, lipstick, rouge, and powder. The effort was exhausting, and everyone lay down again.

The sun reached its zenith. No sound broke the stillness except the buzzing of flies and an occasional bird call. The Salvadorans drifted in and out of consciousness. One young woman, delirious from dehydration and heatstroke, suddenly cried out. "Please God,

I don't want to suffer any more!" Rivera heard her. He crawled toward his victim, dragging a large stick.

"You want to die now?" He looked at the others. They cringed under his gaze. "It's better to die now," he said. "The ones who live longest will only suffer the most." The young woman made a croaking noise. Rising unsteadily to his knees, Rivera swung the stick and hit her in the face.

Less than three miles away, the Border Patrol was just beginning a search for survivors. It had taken them almost a day to get one of the captured Salvadorans to admit that others were still out there. The father-coyote and the two university students had stoically refused to talk, believing it disloyal to turn the others in. But the stocky housewife, who'd hitched a ride into town with the younger coyote before he disappeared and she was caught, finally broke down. In tears, she told two Border Patrol agents the truth. They put her in a four-wheel-drive land cruiser and raced south to where she said she remembered coming out to the road. By the time they got there, Berta had changed her mind about helping with the search. The border patrolmen had to lock her in the back and go looking on their own.

The sun had set when they found the men, lying near a power-pole line about a mile west of the highway. One had smeared tooth-paste on his face to protect it, and, in near-darkness, the border patrolman saw a white flash. Earlier, the men had tried make a signal by igniting a pole with spray-deodorant. The attempt failed, and some then found relief by burying their heads in the sand. They'd been there for several hours when, in the late afternoon, two jets flew low overhead. Fighter pilots from Davis-Monthan Air Force Base in Tucson often practiced over Organ Pipe National Monument. The Salvadoran men thought the planes were looking for them, and it gave them hope. All but three survived.

The women who stayed with Carlos Rivera fared worse. The Border Patrol did not find them until 10 the following morning, July 6. They were still lying where the coyotes had left them, not two miles from the road. Seven of ten were dead, including the three Huezo sisters. The survivors said Rivera had beaten all the women he could reach before he died. They also insisted they'd seen him rape and strangle two of the Huezo girls. The state medical examiner, however, contradicted their reports. He determined that all the Salvadorans except Chalatenango had died of sunstroke and dehydration. According to his report, the only sign of sexual activity was Rivera's open fly; the girls' bodies were unmolested.

The two women who had left the group at nightfall escaped, and Don Cruz was never found. The thirteen other survivors were arrested. After they recovered, the Border Patrol moved them to a jail in Tucson, 140 miles away, to await deportation hearings. Their story made national headlines, and many Americans were appalled to learn that, after all they had suffered, the U.S. government was planning to send the survivors back to El Salvador. In Tucson, a small group of lawyers and church people came together to prevent that from happening.

MAY 4, 1981

Jim and Pat Corbett were country people at heart. Their property, at the end of a rutted dirt street in north Tucson, in many ways resembled the ranch they would have preferred. It had a corral for Pat's mule Boo, a pen for Jim's goats, a chicken coop, a garden, and dogs and cats and geese roaming in the yard. The Corbetts lived in the main house, a one-story, beige adobe, and they rented out the other house and four trailers scattered around the property. Shaded by mesquite and chinaberry trees, nearly in the shadow of the Santa Catalina mountains, Flanwill Street was probably as close to country living as one could hope for in a city of half-a-million.

On the evening of May 4, the Corbetts had a visitor. Frank Shutts, a member of the Claremont, California, Friends Meeting, was in Tucson to gain support for El Centro de Paz. The Peace Center was an organization founded by Shutts to promote understanding between people on both sides of the border. He told the Corbetts that plans were underway to start a Friends' center in Hermosillo, the capital of Sonora.

Shutts was traveling from one Quaker Meeting to another, much as John Woolman had done, seeking support from the people most likely to give it—other Quakers. Members of the Religious Society of Friends were encouraged to work on each other's projects: Jim Dudley, another Quaker, a mutual friend of the Corbetts and Frank Shutts, was also due in this evening. Dudley had borrowed a van from Jim Corbett to help set up a work camp in the Sierra Madre,

east of Hermosillo. Dudley and his wife and a group of North
Americans were going to spend the summer helping the villagers of
La Iglesia build themselves a church.

While they waited for Dudley, Corbett took Frank Shutts out
back to show him the goats. Corbett had taken up goatherding in
1977, after his forced retirement from cattle ranching. He had a
theory that goats were much better suited to desert living than cows.
In recent years, he'd spent time with semi-nomadic Baja Californi-
ans, studying and writing about their goat-cheese economy. Mexican
goats were tough little creatures, but they didn't give as much milk
as the American barnyard varieties. Corbett introduced several Nu-
bian goats into the Baja strains, hoping to develop a goat that was
both hardy and generous with milk. But the Baja goatherds complained that the cross-breeds were still too susceptible to disease.
Corbett also helped set up a cooperative to share the bucks. After
he left, the mistrust among families resurfaced and the cooperative
fell apart.

Contemplating these problems, Corbett and Shutts were silent
for a minute. Corbett's face was long and thin, made longer by a
narrow, downturned nose and a goatee. The skin around his pale
blue eyes had a slight Oriental fold, which Corbett said was a sign of
his Plains-Indian blood. He wore utilitarian plastic-framed glasses,
and his mousey-brown hair was short. Corbett was 46 years old. His
ruddy face was etched with the evidence of a lifetime of work in the
sun.

Corbett told Shutts about his goat-group, a co-op of friends and
former students from his days as a teacher at a Quaker high school
in California. They took turns milking, a difficult chore for Corbett's
arthritic hands. His fingers and toes curled up over each other like
limp tree roots, and he had to wear canvas shoes with holes cut in
the sides to accommodate his misshapen feet. Even so, he got around
well, and he'd learned to hold a pen or a fork between his fingers
and a cup in the crook of his palm. More complicated tasks like
hammering and tying were beyond him; Corbett had probably seen
his last days as a rancher.

The sunset faded behind the Tucson mountains, and Corbett and
Frank Shutts headed back to the house. In the cluttered living room,
Pat Corbett sat reading a science-fiction paperback. She was Jim's
second wife, a few years younger than he, and healthier. Since they

sold the ranch, Pat had supported Jim by working as an arid-lands crops research technician. She jokingly referred to her job as that of a "glorified field hand." On the wall was a picture of Pat doing what she really enjoyed—jumping horses.

The three of them wondered what had happened to Jim Dudley, who by then was late. Tardiness was not like Dudley, a high-school math teacher from Albuquerque. He usually exemplified Quaker ideals of honesty and plain speaking. If Dudley said he would be there, he would be there.

A little after 9, Dudley showed up. He looked tired and upset, but he didn't say what was bothering him right away. He accepted Pat's offer of a sardine-and-Swiss-chard supper, and, while he ate, they talked about the subjects at hand: summer work camps, El Centro de Paz, and goats. Corbett asked about the van Dudley had borrowed. It had been very useful, Dudley said, and the work camp needed one. Corbett said he was willing to donate the van, which had been a gift to him for his goat project, but it was against Mexican law for Americans to bring vehicles into the country and leave them. Corbett suggested ways of getting around the law while technically remaining within it. He thought that would be enough to satisfy both Mexican bureaucrats and Quakers concerned about propriety.

Finally, Jim Dudley brought up what was on his mind. Part of the reason he was late, he said, was because he'd picked up a hitch-hiker outside Nogales. He'd just crossed the border, 60 miles south of Tucson, and was heading up the freeway, when he saw someone standing by the side of the road. At first Dudley thought the hitch-hiker was Mexican-American. Then he tried to strike up a conversation and discovered that the fellow spoke only Spanish. Dudley's Spanish was not great, but he understood the hitchhiker enough to learn that his name was Nelson, that he was 20 years old and a citizen of El Salvador. The hitchhiker showed Dudley his Salvadoran identity card, and the two of them chatted amiably until the van got to the Peck Canyon turnoff, 12 miles up the road. The Border Patrol had a roadblock set up there, and, when Dudley pulled over, they arrested his passenger.

"Really?" Jim Corbett said, leaning forward. "What happened?"

Dudley told the story. The Border Patrol had put him in one trailer, the Salvadoran in another, and interrogated them. "At first, the guy came in and asked me what my story was," Dudley said. "I told him the truth—that I picked him up hitchhiking and I thought he was Chicano. The next thing, he came back in and said the Salvadoran had told them that he'd paid me $200 to take him to Tucson. Now, that made me mad. I don't think I said anything to that.

"I don't know how long this went on—maybe a half-hour. Then, we were leaving—they were leading me back to the van, and I didn't know what they were going to do. They had the fellow in handcuffs, and we passed quite close to each other. I could tell by the look he gave me that he wasn't trying to turn me in as a coyote."

Dudley paused. "I wonder what I could have said to get us through," he said. "Made a joke, perhaps. It happened so fast."

Jim Corbett had never had any dealings with the Border Patrol personally, but, like all southern Arizonans, he'd been through their periodic roadblocks. "Once you're stopped," he assured his friend, "I don't think there's too much you can do."

"Yeah, but if I'd known where that checkpoint was, I could have gone around it," Dudley said. "I suppose I could have gotten off the freeway as soon as I picked him up. I could have gone the other way."

Jim Corbett stroked his goatee with his bent hand. He tried to think if there were some way Dudley could have winged it and gotten through. Definitely not, he decided. It would take a lot of advance planning to run somebody around an immigration checkpoint.

Dudley accepted his friend's judgment. Corbett was known among his friends and family for having a quick, analytical mind. Some of his teachers remembered him as one the brightest students they had ever had. After graduating from high school in Wyoming, he got a full scholarship to Colgate, graduated with a degree in philosophy in three years, and went on to receive a master's in philosophy from Harvard in one. (His mother, an Ozark horsewoman, said Jim didn't like her to brag about his 175 IQ.) Corbett took his East Coast education and went home to the west. A contemplative, outdoor life appealed to him, and he figured he could ponder philosophical questions on the back of a horse as easily as anywhere else.

From his years of ranching down near Bisbee, Corbett knew that Mexicans frequently crossed the border to find work. Dudley's hitchhiker, however, he understood to be in a different situation. A war was going on in El Salvador, which in itself would be reason to leave. Corbett had also read about random murders and disappearances—things that made him think El Salvador was a terrible place, one he'd never want to visit. Central American politics weren't a particular concern of his, and he didn't know too much about the causes of the war. But he did have compassion for its victims. His friend's experience affected him more than any news story he had read.

Now that he thought about it, Corbett remembered something that had happened the previous summer. Thirteen Salvadorans, abandoned by coyotes, had died in Organ Pipe National Monument. According to the papers, the Salvadorans were respectable, middle-class people. Some of the women had been found wearing high-heeled shoes. It struck Corbett as unlikely that they had all tried to march across a desert to find jobs.

Frank Shutts had read a little more about El Salvador than either the Corbetts or Jim Dudley. He told them what he knew.

El Salvador was a tiny, crowded, desperately poor nation in the "delicate waist of America," as Chilean poet Pablo Neruda called it. In 1976, the United Nations had found that 73 percent of all Salvadoran children under the age of 5 were malnourished. Eighty percent of rural families lived in substandard houses, without electricity or running water. Since the Spanish conquest, the country had been dominated by an oligarchy of wealthy landowners, and since the 1920s, fourteen families had controlled every sector of society, including the army. The vast majority of people were illiterate, landless peasants. In the 1930s, El Salvador's military rulers quelled a peasant uprising by slaughtering more than 30,000 people. They were determined to rule the country with an iron fist.

Against this backdrop of repression, the Catholic Church in the 1970s introduced in El Salvador *comunidades de base*, or Christian base communities. Their purpose was to bring together small groups of people to worship, learn to read and write, discuss health care, and generally improve the condition of their lives. Dom Hélder Câmera, a pacifist Brazilian priest, was one of the first priests to establish Christian base communities in the 1960s. Then, in the early 1970s, the Catholic Church in Latin America underwent a historic realignment, toward the poor and away from the wealthy and powerful. The introduction of liberation theology, as this new position of the church was called, was a tremendous threat to the Salvadoran government. The country's military rulers knew their control of the situation was, at best, tenuous. Urban guerrillas were already active, kidnapping members of the oligarchy to finance their campaigns, and working people were staging strikes and marches to demand better wages and conditions. The government wasted no time in branding church workers and labor organizers as communists and in league with the guerrillas. Some Christian base communities became pockets of popular resistance, but others remained nonviolent, and the government was unable or unwilling to distinguish between guerrillas and those who wanted to work peacefully for change. Soldiers were ordered to shoot protest marchers in the streets of San Salvador. Students, foreign agricultural technicians, and human-rights activists suffered grisly deaths. Monsignor Oscar Arnulfo Romero, the popular Archbishop of San Salvador, was the country's leading advocate of peaceful reform during the strife-torn years of the late '70s. In his weekly Sunday sermons, broadcast over the radio to all parts of the country, Archbishop Romero demanded a full accounting of human-rights abuses and an end to the bloodshed on both sides. On March 23, 1980, he went too far, saying:

I would like to make a special appeal to the members of the army, and specifically to the ranks of the National Guard, the police, and the military. Brothers, each one of you is one of us. We are the same people. The peasants you kill are your own brothers and sisters. When you hear the voice of the man commanding you to kill, remember instead the voice of God: Thou Shalt Not Kill. God's law must prevail. No soldier is obliged to obey an order contrary to the law of God. There is still time for you to obey your conscience, even in the face of a sinful command to kill.

The Church, defender of the rights of God, of the law of God, and the dignity of each human being, cannot remain silent in the presence of such abominations. In the name of God, in the name of our tormented people whose cries rise up to Heaven, I beseech you, I beg you, I command you, *stop the repression.*

The next day, Romero was celebrating Mass at the Convent of the Good Shepherd in San Salvador. From the back of the chapel, someone shot him once through the heart. Calling for soldiers to lay down their arms was, in the eyes of the government, a subversive act.

The Salvadoran government would have fallen, as Nicaragua's had the year before, if President Jimmy Carter had not started sending military hardware and advisors in the summer of 1980. (Before he was killed, Romero had written to President Carter, begging him not to do this.) Carter's policy was stepped up under the Reagan administration, which saw the conflict completely in terms of an East-West power struggle. According to a 1980 Reagan administration document called the Santa Fe Group Paper, U.S. foreign policy in Latin America needed to counter the influence of liberation theology, and the U.S. government began training Salvadoran soldiers and shipping millions of dollars worth of weapons to the Salvadoran government. At the same time, it still refused to recognize fleeing Salvadorans as refugees from a war zone. They were classified as illegal aliens and deported. Frank Shutts told his friends a story he'd heard about a planeload of deported Salvadorans who were massacred upon arrival in San Salvador in December. It was done, he said, as an example to anyone else who might be considering leaving the country.

In 1981 documentation on the fate of deported Salvadorans was difficult to come by. The only people who knew what was happening were those directly involved. Indirect confirmation was available from Zoila Serpas, an Arizona resident and the aunt of José Napoleón Duarte (who, with U.S. backing, was appointed President of the Salvadoran junta in 1980 and then elected President in 1984). Serpas told researchers in late 1981 that she had heard testimony from deportees that some forty people had been massacred when their plane arrived in San Salvador.

The best documented case of a deportee being murdered upon return to El Salvador was that of Santana Chirino Amaya. The 24-year-old man, deported from Laredo, Texas, in June 1981, was found decapitated near the Salvadoran bathing resort of Amulupapa two months later. A 14-year-old friend found with him had also been tortured and decapitated. Professor Blaise Bonpane, a Central American expert at California State University, estimated to the *New York Times* in 1981 that between 5 and 10 percent of deportees were executed upon return to El Salvador, "because the government has something on them, a member of a union or something." The U.S. government denied that any deportees were meeting violent ends.

Corbett was confused. Why would the United States be deporting anyone back to a place like that? He thought perhaps it was some sort of bureaucratic mixup—a case of the right hand not knowing what the left was doing. "There must be some way to intervene for these people," he said.

The conversation ended on the assumption that nothing much could be done for the captured hitchhiker. Dudley had to catch a late bus to Albuquerque. Frank Shutts took him to the station, and the Corbetts went to bed.

MAY 5, 1981

Jim Corbett woke up knowing he had to do something. "I figured I should find out if the guy was likely to be murdered, or what," he said later. He called the Border Patrol, and then the Border Patrol's parent agency, the Immigration and Naturalization Service. Both offices told him they did not give out any information on detainees. Corbett next tried Manzo Area Council, an organization that he'd read protected the rights of illegals. The secretary there said Father Ricardo Elford might be able to help. Corbett wrote down "Father Alfred" and the phone number of Picture Rocks, a Redemptorist retreat in the hills west of Tucson.

When Corbett reached him, Father Elford was on his way out. Fourteen Salvadorans had been arrested on the Papago Indian Reservation that morning, and Father Elford was going down to see what he could do. Margo Cowan and Guadalupe Castillo, Manzo's director and staff paralegal, were already there trying to arrange bond. Corbett discovered that if he wanted to help Dudley's hitchhiker, he would have to do it himself.

Father Elford told Corbett he would need to know both the hitchhiker's full name and where he was being held before the Border Patrol would let anyone talk to him. Corbett would also have to present a government form saying the alien had legal representation. Father Elford offered to bring over the form, called a G-28, and Corbett accepted.

Now the problem was getting information. Father Elford had given Corbett a number to call, but, from his morning's experience, Corbett didn't think the Border Patrol would tell him anything. Then he remembered his name is the same as a former mayor's, a man from a locally prominent family. Corbett called the Border Patrol, and, in the most authoritative voice he could muster, said, "This is Jim Corbett here in Tucson, and I need the name of the Salvadoran you picked up late yesterday at the Peck Canyon roadblock. His name, and where he's being held." It worked. The border patrolman looked up the Salvadoran's name and told Corbett he was being held at the Santa Cruz County Jail.

Father Ricardo Elford, an Anglo priest who spoke Spanish, arrived at Corbett's house. He was small and thin, like Corbett, but his skin was pale and his hair—what was left of it—was white. He wore black horn-rimmed glasses and street clothes. Father Elford was pastor of the Santa Rosa Mission, at the Yaqui Indian village in town. Refugees were a recent concern, he told Corbett, dating back only to January, when he had been asked to visit a jailed Salvadoran girl. Since then, he'd been working almost full-time with Manzo Area Council.

Father Elford explained the procedure. First, Corbett had to make sure the hitchhiker didn't sign a voluntary departure form, which was basically an admission he was here illegally and an agreement to be deported. If the Salvadoran had already signed one, he could write out a retraction, but, Father Elford said, the Border Patrol usually ignored a retraction unless it was in the hands of a lawyer. The G-28 was supposed to prevent the Border Patrol from deporting people without their lawyer knowing. In Father Elford's experience, G-28s weren't always honored, either.

He gave Corbett a blue form, already signed by Margo Cowan. Corbett had to get the Salvadoran's signature and then file the paper with the INS. He took it and set off for Nogales.

Santa Cruz County Jail was located near the border, about 5 miles east of Nogales. Corbett had never been there before, but he went in and presented the G-28 as if he'd done it all his life. The jailers must have thought he was a lawyer, because they put him in a little room and brought the Salvadoran to him.

The man they brought was not the hitchhiker. He was another Salvadoran named Nelson. (Corbett later learned that English names were relatively common in Central America.) Corbett talked with this other Nelson for about twenty minutes and discovered that a Salvadoran woman was also being held in the Santa Cruz jail. He went out and asked to see her but was refused because he didn't know her name. The guards did allow Corbett to visit with Dudley's hitchhiker, and, by doing some fast talking, Corbett was also able to see a third man, an engaging young Salvadoran named Enrique Molina Parada.

Molina had been arrested and deported once before, and he knew a little about his rights. He told Corbett he had no intention of signing a voluntary deportation form. He'd just gotten a letter from his mother, and she'd written about a whole planeload of refugees being shot at the airport. "Whatever you do, don't let them send you back here," she wrote.

Molina was from San Miguel, a city in eastern El Salvador that was a center of fighting between guerrillas and government troops. He described for Corbett some of the things going on there. A friend had been taken from his home in the middle of the night, tortured, and dismembered. Enrique said he'd fled the country with his sister-in-law and her cousin, both of whom had been arrested with him. He asked Corbett to find out where they were.

Corbett went out again and asked for G-28 forms for Molina and the other Nelson. We don't have any here, the jailer said. Corbett went to the Border Patrol office, next to the international fence in downtown Nogales, and asked for the G-28s. We're all out, the agent behind the desk told him.

"Well, I guess I can just make my own," Corbett said.

"No, wait a minute," the border patrolman said.

Corbett sat down to wait. He watched the Border Patrol agents go in and out. Most ignored him, but one, an older man with graying blond hair, stopped to talk. Corbett couldn't tell for sure, but he thought the agent might be in a position of authority. Corbett brought up the women Molina had told him about, and, to his surprise, the border patrolman revealed where they were being held. They were at a place called House of Samuel, a detention center run for the INS by Evangelical Christians in Sahuarita, a little town about 20 miles south of Tucson. (Less than a month later, Corbett met a Salvadoran who had also encountered this Border Patrol agent. Instead of arresting him, the officer let him go back to Mexico.)

After about half an hour, Corbett asked again for the G-28s. The agent behind the desk made him wait a few more minutes and then finally produced two. Corbett drove back to the jail and asked to see Enrique Molina and Nelson. Again, he was told he'd have to wait.

Another half-hour went by. It was getting near three, and Corbett had to be back in Tucson to file the G-28s by five. He asked if he might finally see the Salvadorans.

"Who was it you were waiting for?" the jailer asked.

Corbett told him.

"Oh, you wanted to see those guys? The Border Patrol took them 20 or 30 minutes ago. They're gone."

MID-MAY 1981

In a span of less than two weeks, Jim Corbett had gone from hardly knowing that Salvadoran refugees existed to total immersion in their lives. What had at first appeared to him as benign neglect on the part of the immigration service now looked more like a deliberate effort to deny these people access to legal aid and to ship them, as quickly as possible, back to El Salvador. The realization that his government would be doing such a thing was shocking. Corbett knew that the situation required him to act. He had to try to save as many refugees as he could.

The Corbetts got a $4,500 lien on one of their trailers and, with Manzo's help, bailed four women and a baby out of jail. The refugees stayed in a converted-garage apartment on the side of Jim and Pat's house. One of these first refugees to stay at the Corbetts' was Molina's sister-in-law. She had been held at House of Samuel with two other women, Gladis and Isabel, and Isabel's baby. They were all friends, students from San Salvador. The fourth woman didn't fit in with their group. She was a *campesina*, a peasant, from the area outside San Miguel. Her name was Ana Daisie.

One evening, Ana Daisie came over to talk to Jim and Pat. She was in her early twenties, small and thin, with European features and coloring. Corbett offered her a beer, and, by her reaction, he could tell he'd insulted her. Reputable Salvadoran women do not drink, he learned.

In a soft voice, Ana Daisie told what had happened to her family. The big cotton farmer next door killed their cow; "He sprayed us [with pesticides] along with everything else." Troops came to the village and killed people. Most traumatic of all, Ana had watched her sister go slowly insane. The girl just withdrew into herself, quit talking, and quit reacting to anything. Fearful that the same thing might happen to her, Ana left.

She and a girlfriend made it to Mazatlán, Mexico, a west-coast tourist town that also happened to be on a main route north. Immigration officers got on the bus there, demanding to see papers. Ana Daisie kept insisting she was Mexican, but they didn't believe her and forced her and the other woman off. One of the immigration agents said he knew that Ana and her friend were Salvadoran, but it didn't matter, because he could get them a job.

Ana managed to convince the Mexican agents to let her go to the bathroom. Quickly, she went in and arranged her hair in a different style, changed clothes, and put on makeup. Then she walked out, right past the agents who were still holding her friend, and up on to the bus. She sat down in the seat behind the driver and struck up a conversation with him. The immigration officials, realizing they'd been tricked, rushed on, looked at the seat where she'd been, scanned the bus, and rushed off again. Ana escaped. Her friend did not.

Trouble followed Ana north. In Nogales, she was arrested and held in solitary for six weeks at the Santa Cruz County Jail. "They kept trying to break me," she said, "they threatened me with all kinds of things if I didn't sign a voluntary departure form. But I wouldn't." She was the woman the other prisoners had told Corbett about the day he went to the jail—the one he couldn't see because he didn't know her name.

Ana had a brother in Los Angeles, but she wasn't allowed to call him. She couldn't post bond and would have been deported, had she not been brought before the immigration judge the same day that Margo Cowan and Lupe Castillo were there putting up bonds for the women at House of Samuel. The judge asked Ana Daisie, "Do you have representation?" Before she could say no, Cowan jumped up and said, "She is being represented by Manzo, your honor!"

During her stay at the Corbetts', Ana spent a lot of time talking with Jim. She was less sophisticated about Salvadoran politics than the city women who were there, and occasionally she'd say things that offended them. Once Corbett asked her why she hadn't sought asylum in Costa Rica, a democratic country much closer to El Salvador. Ana replied: "I couldn't do that. They're communists in Costa Rica!"

The first two weeks in Tucson were difficult for Ana Daisie. She cried a lot, and Corbett thought she might be on the verge of a nervous breakdown. He saw that getting refugees to a safe place did not end their troubles, but at least it was a start. As she'd demonstrated in Mazatlán, Ana was determined to survive.

In the next few months, Corbett was to discover that Ana's attitude and experiences were typical of refugee women. Only the most resourceful and most persistent survived. The rest ended up forced into prostitution in Mexico, deported, or dead.

MAY 21, 1981

At 5 o'clock, a small group of demonstrators gathered in the plaza in front of the federal building in downtown Tucson. They carried hand-lettered signs and walked slowly in a circle. Stop persecution of clergy in Central America, read one sign. End U.S. intervention in El Salvador, read another. More people arrived, took up signs, and the circle grew. Soon fifteen or twenty had assembled in the ninety-degree heat. Rush-hour drivers, backed up at the light on Congress Street, stared from inside their air-conditioned cars.

The prayer vigil began at 5:20. Father Elford handed out printed sheets, and the protestors put down their signs and stood quietly. They took turns reciting the liturgy, which this week was mostly quotes from Latin American liberation theologians. One, from Bishop Mortimer Arias, of the Bolivian Methodist Evangelical Church, said, "The God whom we know in the Bible is a liberating God, a God who destroys myths and alienations, a God who intervenes in history in order to break down the structures of injustice and who raises up prophets in order to point out the way of justice and mercy." Father Elford, wearing a straw hat, read from Luke: "He that hath two coats, let him impart to him who hath none; and he that hath meat, let him do likewise." The next verse, Matthew 6:24, was read first in Spanish by a Salvadoran, then in English. "No one can serve two masters," the verse ended, "for either he will hate the one and love the other, or he will be devoted to the one and despise the other. You cannot serve God and mammon. . . ."

The vigil over, Father Elford thanked everyone for coming—especially during the hot weather—and the group began to disperse. Soon only a handful of people remained. John M. Fife, pastor of Southside United Presbyterian Church, helped Father Elford put the signs in his car. Fife was 41, a few years younger than the priest. A tall, thin man, he wore jeans and cowboy boots. Although originally from western Pennsylvania, Fife had adopted the Arizona style of wearing jewelry. His belt buckle and watchband were silver with turquoise inlay. As soon as the vigil ended, he lit a Pall Mall.

Fife and Elford had started these vigils together. In December 1980, when they heard about the murder of four American church workers in El Salvador, the two men decided they had to do something. "The only thing we could think of to do," Fife recalled, "was what I assume people of faith have always thought of first, and that is, 'Let's pray.'" The vigils, held every Thursday afternoon since mid-February, had become a place for local church and legal workers to meet and talk about refugees.

By his own admission, John Fife could barely find El Salvador on a map before 1981. He didn't speak Spanish, and he had had no personal contact with Salvadorans. But he learned from the people who came to the vigils. Margo Cowan and Lupe Castillo, of Manzo Area Council, opened his eyes to the refugees in jails around Tucson, and Fife found out that the Salvadorans would be released without bail if he wrote letters saying his congregation would sponsor a certain family. He wrote a dozen such letters during the first months of '81. Then, in April and May, the bonds started going up—first to $500, then $1,000, then $1,500, then $2,000 per Salvadoran. Bonds for Mexicans stayed at $500.

Fife was surprised at the increase. Margo Cowan and Lupe Castillo, who had been protesting INS practices for years, were not. Manzo Area Council, originally formed in the '60s as part of the War on Poverty, was until 1982 the only organization in Tucson representing undocumented people at low or no cost. Manzo began hearing about the arrests and deportations of Salvadoran refugees from its Mexican clients. By mid-1978, the council was representing a steady flow of Central Americans.

Several early attenders at the vigils could trace their involvement with Salvadoran refugees to the 1980 tragedy in Organ Pipe National Monument. Journalist and lawyer Dr. Gary MacEoin, a bearded Irishman in his seventies, was one. MacEoin spoke five languages, had written more than twenty books, and was considered an expert on the church and society in Latin America. Soon after moving to Tucson in 1974, MacEoin and his wife met Dr. Paul David Sholin, the pastor of St. Mark's Presbyterian Church. Sholin was a missionary's son, born in Argentina and raised in Spain during the '30s. He and MacEoin became good friends, and Sholin offered MacEoin office space at St. Mark's. In 1979, they had met Archbishop Romero at a meeting of Latin American bishops in Puebla, Mexico. Sholin and McEoin also helped organize the effort to prevent the deportation of the desert survivors.

St. Mark's interest in refugees had begun more than 20 years before, when Sholin signed up for a planeload of Cubans who were escaping Fidel Castro. MacEoin and Sholin shared a particular concern for Spanish-speaking refugees, and throughout the 1970s the church helped resettle Chileans fleeing military rule. In July 1980, Sholin pledged $2,500 of St. Mark's discretionary fund to bond the desert survivors out of jail. The Roman Catholic diocese of Phoenix donated another $2,000, and Pima County Supervisor David Yetman added $500, to make the $5,000 total bond. After being released, the thirteen survivors applied for political asylum. None had yet been deported.

John Fife was not involved with the efforts to care for the desert survivors, but he had met Dave Sholin earlier. In 1970, Fife called Sholin from Canton, Ohio, where he'd first worked as a minister, to ask about Southside Presbyterian. Southside was a small, poor, racially mixed congregation in need of a pastor—just what Fife was looking for. Sholin told him that the Presbytery (an elected body with power similar to a Catholic bishop's) was planning to close Southside and merge the congregation with another one, and he offered Fife the assistant pastorship at St. Mark's. John's wife, Marianne, wanted him to take that job. Fife wanted to be his own boss. He convinced the Presbytery to give him two years at Southside, but convincing Marianne to move into the barrio with him was more difficult. "If you go down that road now, it's going to be like that for the rest of our lives," she told him. The Fifes later described this as the most serious dispute of their marriage. John won out, but only after he promised Marianne that she could pick the next place they lived.

Ten years later, with one son going away to college and the other entering high school, the Fifes agreed that it was time for a change. John thought he'd done all he could do for Southside. The congregation had grown from less than 30 to 125, and many members were active in the community. With Father Elford, Fife had held prayer vigils for demonstrators lobbying the city to convert a nearby country club into a neighborhood center. They had also held services for families of prisoners protesting conditions at the state penitentiary in Florence. In 1978, they began their first weekly prayer vigil in front of the federal building, in response to the shooting of a South Tucson boy by a policeman. More than two years later, the Justice Department agreed to open an inquiry into whether the boy's civil rights had been violated. That experience convinced Fife and Father Elford that prayer vigils could work.

Fife had also accomplished some personal goals in Tucson. He had served as the Arizona and New Mexico representative on the Presbyterian national board, the General Assembly Mission Council, for eight years, and as chairman of the Committee on Mission Responsibility Through Investment for six. His committee job was to make sure the investments of the Presbyterian church—a $750 million portfolio—coincided with its ethical position on matters such as human rights and the environment. Fife had established contacts within the hierarchy of the Presbyterian church, as well as with board members of many of the country's major corporations.

By 1980, the Fifes were ready to leave Tucson. John had thought of going back to school to get his doctorate in divinity, and Marianne, a virologist at the University of Arizona Medical Center, wanted to relocate where she, too, could pursue her career. But the appearance of hundreds of Salvadoran refugees in Tucson made them change their plans.

The people who came together at the vigils—Fife, Elford, Margo Cowan, Lupe Castillo, Gary MacEoin, and Dave Sholin, among others—decided they needed a more coordinated approach to the refugee crisis. They also knew it would be easier to raise bond money with an institutional base. Refugees had been a recognized concern of the church since at least the end of World War II, and they decided to approach the Tucson Ecumenical Council. The TEC represented more than fifty Protestant and Catholic churches, with committees on faith and worship, church unity, arms control, and community social action. In mid-May, Dave Sholin made an impassioned speech to the social action committee, asking them to form a task force. The TEC agreed. Mike Smith, assistant pastor at St. Mark's and president of the TEC in 1981, was appointed chairman, and Timothy Nonn, a young seminary student at St. Mark's, was given the job of project director. Nonn began organizing the first major meeting of the TEC task force on Central America, to be held at the Redemptorist Fathers' Picture Rocks retreat in late June.

MAY 30, 1981

From Father Elford, Jim Corbett knew of the existence of the TEC task force, but he was not initially a member. Corbett preferred to go his own way. He visited with Salvadorans in jail and learned about their past experiences and their treatment at the hands of the INS. He wrote long letters to other Quakers and Quaker meetings around the country, explaining the refugees' desperate need for legal and social services. Although he did not specifically ask for money in these "Dear Friends" letters, people sent it. Corbett used their donations to post bonds and to pay bills for the refugees staying at his house.

After three weeks at Jim and Pat's, Ana Daisie felt well enough to move on. Corbett drove her over to her brother's house in Los Angeles, accompanied by a 21-year-old Salvadoran named Rubén, a volunteer at Manzo Area Council. Rubén and Corbett planned to visit two big detention centers in southern California: the SPAN women's facility in Pasadena and the Service Processing Center at El Centro, a men's jail in the southeast corner of the state. They suspected they might find at least twelve refugees, most of whom had been spirited out of jails around Nogales and Tucson without Manzo's knowledge. Corbett had copies of G-28s already signed and filed with the INS. Rubén carried a pocket tape-recorder. He used it to listen to music, but he also brought it into the prisons to document whatever happened.

Rubén was a former journalism student at the University of San Salvador. A member of a student's union who also held a government job, Rubén felt himself in danger and fled to Mexico City in October 1980. He found a job and a place to stay, but soon his landlord found out he was Salvadoran and threatened to turn him in unless Rubén gave him all his belongings and his next paycheck. Rubén gave the landlord what he had and headed north. In January 1981, he came into the United States by walking across the Organ Pipe National Monument. Rubén stayed underground for a while, until he heard that Manzo Area Council could help him apply for political asylum. He filed his request with the INS and was released on his own recognizance. Rubén wanted to use his temporary legal status to help other Salvadorans who were not so fortunate. This would be the first time inside a detention center for either him or Corbett.

On the way to El Centro, Rubén told Corbett what life had been like in El Salvador. His description of Archbishop Romero's funeral was later recorded by a TEC interviewer.

There were about 10,000 of us in the plaza in front of the cathedral. They were giving the Mass, and all of a sudden a bomb went off. A lot of times they throw publicity bombs [scattering leaflets], but then they started firing and we all started running. People fell and we ran over them. The exchange of bullets lasted five minutes, no more. They said it was from the palace; in front of the cathedral is the national palace. There were a lot of bombs, but I think most people died from being trampled and suffocating. We wanted to go into the cathedral for cover, and we went in where there were children —many people—dead. The cathedral was too small for the crowd. There wasn't much air. We were surrounded for about two hours, and they were shooting at the cathedral.

In all, thirty people were killed that day.

Corbett and Rubén drove into the detention center parking lot. It was about noon, and a few palm trees cast small shadows on the asphalt and dry grass. The prison was a three-hour drive from Los Angeles, on the northern outskirts of the agricultural town of El Centro. A tall fence with barbed-wire on top surrounded the twelve-building compound, the last stop for almost every male Central American arrested on immigration violations in the Southwest. Between three and four hundred men were in there at any given time, about half of whom were OTMs (Border Patrol jargon for Other Than Mexicans). Mexicans were usually put across the border the same day they were caught, unless the INS wanted to hold them as witnesses against a coyote.

Corbett stated their business to the speaker box, and the doors unlocked automatically to let them into the visitor's center. Corbett went over to the counter and presented three G-28s to the agent in charge. He was a heavy-set man in his mid-forties named J.E. Aguirre. Two of the forms were for the men Corbett had met in the Santa Cruz County Jail on May 5. The third was for Alejandro Hernández, a Salvadoran who, after deciding not to apply for asylum, had been arrested in Phoenix.

Enrique Molina and Alejandro Hernández were brought into the room. Corbett asked where Nelson was. Aguirre checked his papers and said there was no record of him. Corbett questioned Aguirre some more. Aguirre insisted he didn't know where Nelson was, and there was no way to find out. Enrique Molina, who spoke some English, broke in. "He was here," Molina told Corbett, "but they sent him back to El Salvador."

When he heard that, Aguirre ordered the Salvadoran to shut up. He told his guard to take them away. He then informed Corbett that he would not be allowed to speak to Molina, Hernández, or anyone else at El Centro.

"But we've come all the way from Tucson to see them," Corbett protested. "I even called ahead to confirm your visiting hours, and they told me I'd be able to speak to these men." Aguirre was adamant. Corbett tried a different tack. "I'm a personal friend. I have news from their families." Aguirre still refused. Under no circumstances was he going to let Corbett talk to the prisoners.

Corbett took out a piece of paper and wrote down what had happened. He started to read it to Aguirre and the other guard, asking them to let him know if there were any mistakes or things they wanted to add.

"I'm not going to listen to this," Aguirre said—and walked out. Corbett waited until he came back, finished reading, and asked Aguirre if there was anyone else at El Centro—the director maybe —whom he could talk to. Corbett was upset because Manzo had had legal representation for the young man who had been deported. Aguirre, saying nothing, glanced at Rubén, who had been standing in silence the whole time. He noticed the Salvadoran was holding a tape recorder. Rubén quickly handed the machine to Corbett, who told Aguirre he was ready to go.

"Not till you give me that tape, you're not," Aguirre said. He ordered his guard to lock the door.

For half an hour, Aguirre kept them there. Corbett told him the tape was his personal property, and, if Aguirre wanted it, he would have to take it by force. "You're trying to extort evidence of INS agents denying Salvadorans their legal rights," Corbett said. Finally, Aguirre made a phone call. Within a few minutes, he unlocked the door, and told Corbett and Rubén they could leave.

When they were safely in the car, Corbett discovered that the tape was blank. Rubén had been too terrified to push the button.

JUNE 4, 1981

Every Thursday, Los Cabreros Andantes (which Corbett translated as the goatherds-errant) met at Jim and Pat's house. They arranged a milking schedule and discussed such questions as who was going to trim the goats' feet or clean the pen, but these weekly meetings were really more social than anything else. Most of the twelve to fifteen milkers were friends, former students, or neighbors of the Corbetts. One sold candles in the DeGrazia shops; another was a sculptor who lived in a geodesic dome. They took turns at the twice-daily chore of milking White Queen, Roma, and Salomé. In the spring, after kidding, each goat gave over a gallon a day: plenty for the milkers, their families, and the Corbetts.

After the meeting was over this Thursday, two members of the goat-group stayed to visit with Jim and Pat. One was an old friend of the Corbetts, a Quaker from Berkeley, California, named Ann Russell. Eleven years before, Russell had been Corbett's student at John Woolman School. Jim and Pat had had the students come live on their ranch in southeastern Arizona while they learned about desert survival, anthropology, and philosophy. They had grown gardens, built pit houses, learned to ride, and gone on goatwalks.

Goatwalking was Jim Corbett's answer to modern society. He began the practice in the mid-'60s, when he and Pat operated a family ranch near Florence. Corbett went out for weeks in the wilderness, subsisting entirely on goat's milk, prickly-pear fruit, mesquite beans, and whatever else he could forage. He took no clock, radio, book, or papers, forcing himself just to exist and observe. Nomadic pastoralism, as Corbett called it, fulfilled his ideal of a simple, harmless life—a way for people to live in harmony with nature, rather than in dominance over it. During the 1970s, Corbett developed a complete philosophy of goatwalking. He wrote a long manuscript on the subject that included poetry, practical suggestions for groups of goatwalkers, and discussion on the difficulty of becoming untamed, of giving up dependence on technology and returning to a wild state.

Corbett had an opportunity to witness this difficulty in his students. Even though the teenagers' program was less rigorous—they brought oatmeal, honey, and raisins to eat with the goat's milk—it was a trying experience for them. The solitude, the lack of diversions or entertainment, left them bored and restless. By the end of two weeks in the mountains, the young people had had more than enough of "living in the present without being stoned," as Corbett put it. They had been unable to find water, so the two gallons each student brought went to the goats. That was the hardest part of the trip for Ann Russell. Being Quaker, she was used to silent contemplation, but not to drinking warm goat's milk when thirsty. Pat Corbett knew what to expect and stayed home. "I'll go on goatwalks until the ham-and-cheese sandwiches run out," she said.

Ann Russell stayed on with the Corbetts that summer, becoming, in Pat's words, their "adopted daughter." In 1976, Russell moved to Tucson, and was now finishing her master's in hydrology at the University of Arizona. She lived just a few blocks from the Corbetts.

Joan Warfield taught English as a second language to foreign students at the university. Corbett had met her in Baja a couple of years before, and, like Ann Russell, Warfield had traveled to Spain and Latin America and spoke Spanish well. Both women had met the refugees who'd stayed in Corbett's apartment. Russell took the Salvadorans swimming at a friend's house once, and when they had wanted to go to Mass, Warfield accompanied them to Father Elford's church.

Corbett, Russell, and Warfield had a beer and talked about refugees. Corbett was telling his friends what had happened at El Centro (he later got Congressman Morris Udall to correspond with the INS about the incident) when, a little after 10, the phone rang. It was Gladis, one of the women who'd stayed in the apartment, calling from Phoenix. She said her brother and a friend were holed up in a basement in Nogales, Sonora. They had been there several days now, waiting for an opportunity to enter the United States, and they were starting to get desperate. Gladis was afraid they might take a stupid chance. She wanted to know if Corbett could do anything.

"Well, I don't know," Corbett said. "I suppose I could go down and talk to them." He got the address: Panama 24, in the San Francisco Hills above Canal Street. The two men were in a place next to the *tienda escondida*—the hidden store.

Corbett hung up. "Anybody want to go to Nogales?" he asked.

Pat, who had to work the next day, declined. Corbett, Russell, and Warfield set off for the border.

This was Corbett's first trip into the underworld of the undocumented, where illegal people lived in constant fear. Neither he nor his friends had any idea what to expect.

The border was deserted at midnight, and Warfield drove through darkened streets until they reached the red-light district. Canal Street was unpaved, a single strip lined with seedy bars and nightclubs. A lone taxi waited in front of the faded-pink Tropicana, and a bouncer stood in a doorway, watching the carload of gringos drive slowly by. Corbett got out to ask directions from a group of men loitering in front of the Horseshoe bar. "It's up there," one said, pointing. "Go two blocks and then turn right."

Above Canal Street, the light quickly faded. Corbett, Russell, and Warfield found themselves in a neighborhood of closely packed, wood and corrugated-tin shacks. The streets were steep, rutted paths, running at odd angles. Warfield had to park the car, and the three started knocking on doors. They succeeded only in rousing several large dogs. None of the houses had any numbers on them. Eventually Corbett found a place with a television set flickering and an old woman in the shadows. Corbett asked about the hidden store. She told him it was at the end of the street, down a path, and a flight of steps.

The hidden store, in the tiny front room of an adobe house, was stocked with candy and soda, and such staples as sugar and sardines, for the residents of Panama 24. The proprietress, a middle-aged woman named Doña María, invited her visitors in. "I'll go get the boys," she said.

Carlos and Chico had been sleeping in a dug-out basement. They dressed and came through a hole into the store. Both were in their early twenties, and Chico wore a sleeveless undershirt that showed off his build. Warfield noticed that he sported a glass post in his left ear and that he was much more talkative than his companion.

Before being deported, Chico said, he had lived in the States for almost two years. That explained his streetwise way. He could even put on a Mexican accent, but it had done him no good when a friend's wife got mad at her husband and informed on him. He was picked up and sent to El Corralón (the big corral—an inmate's term for El Centro), where he stayed for almost a month because he refused to sign a voluntary departure form. Then INS guards put him and Carlos in with a bunch of homicidal Cubans, and, believing their lives were in danger, they signed. That had been three weeks before.

The second they hit the ground in San Salvador, Carlos and Chico started hitchhiking, walking, and hopping buses north again. At the U.S. border, they stopped. Both considered themselves lucky to have survived one deportation: Chico said it was common knowledge in El Salvador that people who were sent back often met with violence. So they'd waited, for five days now, in Doña María's basement, hoping to find someone who could help them get safely across.

Chico talked about conditions at home. He said planes flew over groups of people and sprayed poison on them, like animals. He'd heard of massacres in churches where catechism classes were being conducted.

"Who is doing these things?" Ann Russell asked. "Many people in the United States blame the violence on the guerrillas." Russell recorded the conversation in her diary the next morning.

"It's the army," Chico said, "in the form of death squads. They dress in civilian clothes and go knock on people's doors in the middle of the night."

Carlos spoke up. He was a little shy about telling his experiences. He said his brother had joined the guerrillas, so the death squads came to their neighborhood and killed several of his brothers' friends. Carlos's mother begged him to leave, before he became their next victim. Things had gotten very serious, and he didn't want to die. He ran away.

The young men wondered what they should do, and Corbett didn't know what to tell them. Doña María's son, who had come in to the store while Chico was talking, offered his services. He was about 25, with bushy brows and sunken eyes. "He looked like the classic movie villain," Joan Warfield later recalled. Doña María's son said he had lived on the border his entire life, and he knew where all the holes were in the fence. He said he knew a certain hole, behind a shopping center and right next to the railroad tracks, that Mexicans used all the time. It was near a little park, and Carlos and Chico could meet Corbett there after they crossed.

Corbett didn't think the park was such a good idea. If coyotes used it regularly to meet up with clients, the Border Patrol probably kept a close watch on it. Corbett needed to think of a safer meeting place. He did not want the Salvadorans to have to spend much time on the streets of Nogales, where they would be exposed and vulnerable.

Corbett gave Chico his and Manzo's phone numbers. He told the two men to sit tight for a day or two. "We'll be back," he said. "We'll figure something out tomorrow."

JUNE 5, 1981

Sacred Heart Catholic Church sat atop one of the steep hills in Nogales, Arizona, clearly visible from high places in Nogales, Sonora. The Spanish-style tile-roofed building towered over the surrounding one-story school and houses. At midday, Corbett climbed the stone stairs that led up from the street to a small, shady plaza in front of the church. An American flag flew from a pole on the lawn.

The air inside Sacred Heart was cool and smelled faintly of incense. Corbett looked up at the curved white arches and inlaid-wood ceiling. High above the altar, above the red velvet drapery, a figure of Christ stood with his heart glowing and his hands held open at his sides. The church was empty. Corbett sat in one of the pews in back.

He had chosen Sacred Heart as a meeting place for several reasons. It was open, it was an unlikely place for the Border Patrol to have under surveillance, and it was only three blocks from the fence. Earlier in the day, he had gone to Doña María's and told Carlos and Chico to come to the church as soon as they got across. "It's just down the street from McDonald's," he said. "You can't miss it."

Corbett's mind went back to the last time he had been in a Catholic Church, aside from tourist stops at Mexican cathedrals. It had been on Easter, when he was about nine years old. Neither of his parents were particularly religious. They had always encouraged him to think for himself. Corbett remembered when he was in the third or fourth grade, and he learned that the Baptists promised life everlasting. He went home and told his mother he wanted to be a Baptist preacher. She looked at him and said, "You'll get over it."

"You know how hard-shell Baptists are," Gladys Corbett later explained. "Anybody who didn't believe as they did was out, and Jim just couldn't cotton to that." Corbett avoided organized religion for the next twenty years, finally becoming a Quaker because the religion's "testimonies" of truth-telling and nonviolence appealed to him. So did Quakerism's respect for the individual. Their anti-authoritarian attitude got the Quakers in trouble in seventeenth-century England, where the sect was founded by a charismatic preacher named George Fox. More than 15,000 Quakers were imprisoned, and many more had their property confiscated and livelihoods denied for refusing to take off their hats to noblemen, pay tithes to the church, swear oaths, and other such crimes. An estimated 450 were killed as a result of religious persecution.

William Penn established a successful Quaker settlement in the New World, and for a time Friends were influential in the affairs of the colonies. But when it became clear that the colonies planned to go to war against both the British and the Indians, Friends had to withdraw from politics. The Quaker way of decision-making—by consensus, rather than by majority will—and their unwillingness to fight had no place in the founding of a new nation. The Quakers' pacifist convictions were tolerated by the American government, but the sect never again had any real political power. In the nineteenth century, the Evangelical movement took over a branch of Quakerism, and these Friends softened their antiwar stance. Richard Nixon was from this branch of Quakerism. About 30,000 Friends in this country, however, remained "unprogrammed," maintaining that war was never justified and looking to arbitration and consensus-building as ways to resolve conflict. They had no preachers, in keeping with their belief that all people were equal in God's eyes. Their Meetings for Worship consisted of an hour of silent meditation, and anyone moved to speak was allowed. Friends were also encouraged to demonstrate their faith through social concern. Quakers had a joke about a Presbyterian who attended Meeting for the first time. After sitting in silence for twenty minutes, the church-goer turned to his neighbor and whispered, "When does the service begin?"

"As soon as the worship is over," the Quaker replied.

While he waited in Sacred Heart, the Stations of the Cross caught Corbett's eye. He got up to look at the fourteen plaster-of-paris scenes of the crucifixion that were hanging on the church walls. They were done in high-relief: three-dimensional figures, painted in pastel colors, emerged from a flat, blue-sky background. Corbett walked around the church and read the inscriptions. Jesus Takes His Cross. Jesus Falls for the First Time.

Like many convinced (as opposed to birthright) Quakers, Corbett knew little of the Christian roots of his religion. The symbol of the cross was something he had often wondered about. It had always seemed grotesque to him that artists outdid themselves to express Christ's agony. But, as he examined these Stations of the Cross, he became aware of a deeper meaning. He wrote about it in his next "Dear Friends" letter:

Recently, as I struggled to cope emotionally with having become a peripheral witness to the crucifixion of the Salvadoran people, a suspicion grew that the Cross opens a way beyond breakdown—as revelatory depth meaning rather than salvationist egoism. In contrast to ideologies, which we fashion out of words in order to justify ourselves, the way of the Cross is communicated by being lived. It is met in those who point the way with their lives.

In the midst of this agony, underlying defeat, is fulfillment and renewal —neither a noble fiction nor the rhetoric of conciliation, but the lived reality of the Kingdom of Love. The ways of the violent may prosper, but they are like a dream when one awakes.

Corbett's encounter with refugees, and with Christians like Father Elford, had taught him the true meaning of the cross. Inspired by their hope and love, he wrote a poem.

Give me then, my share of pain,
  survivor's grief and unnamed ills,
the slow decay that yet may maim
  and torture years before it kills.
Burn us with their mark of Cain,
  the outlaw brand the powers despise,
and freeze us with the misfit shame
  that touches ice in knowing eyes.
Bind us with the pauper's chain,
  here where life and health are sold
by those who play the money game
  and fashion God of Mammon's gold.
And let our sense be clear and sane,
  unnumbed by drugs or pious lies

unpoisoned by the urge to blame,
        undrained into self-pity's sighs.

Let it be that this, our fate,
        reveals the working of Your grace,
that we can bear the hurt and hate,
        to grow love's realm, in this pain's place.

Carlos and Chico came into the church. They looked lost, blinking until their eyes adjusted to the light. Then they saw Corbett and went over to him.

The three men sat down to wait for Father Elford, who was on his way down from Tucson with Lupe Castillo and Father Pat Lehan, another Redemptorist priest staying at Picture Rocks for the summer. They were bringing I-589s—political asylum requests. Carlos and Chico wanted to apply for political asylum, so that they would have some legal standing with the INS, and Corbett planned to take them in to file their applications. The purpose of doing the paperwork in advance was to show good faith in case they were stopped on the road to Tucson.

The priests and Lupe Castillo arrived. "What are we doing in this part of the church?" Father Elford asked. "Let's go talk to Arnie. There's room in back where we can work."

They went into a dark, narrow passage that led through the sacristy and then around the corner behind the altar. The church office had a bare linoleum floor, vinyl furniture, and pictures of saints and cardinals on the walls. Father Arnie Noriega, a young priest in jogging shoes, came out from behind a metal desk to welcome them. He made a place in a side office for Lupe Castillo, who sat down with Carlos and Chico and began asking questions. Corbett stayed with the priests, who were discussing the refugee situation in Nogales. Father Elford asked if there were any priests on the other side who might be interested in helping.

"Well, there's Father Quiñones," Father Noriega said. Ramón Dagoberto Quiñones was pastor of El Santuario de Nuestra Señora de Guadalupe (the Sanctuary of Our Lady of Guadalupe), one of the largest churches in Nogales, Sonora. According to Father Noriega, Quiñones was no liberation theologian, but he still worked tirelessly for the poor. Dozens of children were fed every day at his church, and Father Quiñones made weekly visits to the federal prison south of town. He no doubt came in contact with Central Americans there.

"He might be able to tell you what their needs are," Father Noriega said. "But I have to warn you, he's kind of a traditionalist. He may not be much help."

Father Quiñones was in his forties and dark-haired, with bow-like lips that curled into a beatific smile. He met his guests in the tiny, book-lined corner office of his church. Father Elford and Corbett wasted no time telling him the purpose of their visit, translating to Father Lehan as they did.

"The situation is very bad," Father Quiñones told them. Central Americans were arriving in Nogales at an alarming rate. He had at least ten of them staying at the church at any given time. Since September 1980, the Mexican government had been arresting Central Americans and deporting them to the Guatemalan border, and, when he went to the prison, Father Quiñones could see that they were in desperate need. But he had to say Mass for the Mexican inmates and wasn't able to spend time with the Central Americans. He needed another priest, ideally from the other side, to go with him to the prison and talk to the refugees. They needed someone to take messages, make phone calls, and get in touch with their relatives. Father Quiñones asked Corbett and Father Elford if they could help.

"Well, I could come down tomorrow," Father Elford said, "but there's no way I can make it every week."

"I can," Corbett said.

"Okay," Father Elford said, "but you're going to have to be a priest. They won't let you in unless you're a priest."

Corbett said he didn't know much about being a priest.

"Just wear black pants, white shirt, and dark shoes and socks," Father Elford said. "They'll know you're either a priest or a waiter."

Father Elford wasn't kidding. Priests and nuns were forbidden to wear religious garb on the street, one of many anticlerical laws passed after the Mexican Revolution. The church nevertheless remained a dominant force in Mexican society. As long as Corbett was with Father Quiñones, it was unlikely that prison officials would question him too closely.

JUNE 6, 1981

Father Quiñones, Father Elford, Father Lehan, and Corbett met at the Sanctuary of Guadalupe the next morning. Since Father Quiñones was scheduled to celebrate Mass with the prisoners at 10 A.M., they left promptly, driving south out of Nogales, past the edge of town where the squatters' shacks began to thin out and the hillsides became speckled with mesquite bushes and dry grass. They came up a hill, and there, across from a filling station, loomed a dirty and monstrous fortress.

El Centro de Prevención y Readaptación Social (the Center for Social Prevention and Readaptation) was a modern prison, built in the monumental style of Mexican public architecture. Reinforced-concrete panels decorated the front of a 40-foot-high angled stone wall, and bright, orange-painted bars gave it an oddly festive look. One of the empty concrete guard boxes had a cross on it. At least a dozen young men, dressed in street clothes, stood at the gate with M-1 carbines slung over their shoulders. Dogs sauntered back and forth on the ground in front of them.

The guards were expecting Father Quiñones, and after a brief introduction, they slid open the tall orange bars for the priests and Corbett. As Padre Jaime, Corbett visited the prison every week for the next two years, and the guards always admitted him without question. Only on the rarest occasions did they pat him down. They commented that he was a strange priest—he never blessed anyone, and he said things like "good luck" when he left the prisoners—but, with Father Quiñones running interference, the commandante left him alone. (Once, the Corbetts were shopping in Nogales and they ran into one of the guards from the prison. Corbett forgot he was a priest and introduced Pat as his wife. The bewildered guard just smiled politely.)

Father Quiñones led the way up the steps to an open-air vestibule. The commandante's office was on the left, and to the right a short corridor led into the entrance to the men's section. A guard was posted at the steel door, across from the room where the Central American men were kept. Father Quiñones asked the guard to let the priests into their cell.

At least two dozen men of various ages were crowded in an open-air room about 30 feet square. The floor and bottom of the wall were covered with prisoners' scratched messages. Someone had gotten on someone else's shoulders to write, high on the wall, "Viva Padre Quiñones."

Father Quiñones began by telling the men, almost all of whom were Salvadoran, that within a few days they would be bused to the Guatemalan border. "There is nothing the church can do about this," he said, "so please don't ask us to help get you out. What we can do is help you get in touch with your family, or your friends, and let them know what has happened to you." Father Quiñones then introduced Corbett and the American priests. He made it clear that they were with the church, to lessen the prisoners' fear that they would supply names and addresses to authorities.

Father Quiñones left to say Mass for the Mexican prisoners, and Corbett handed out the pencils, paper, and envelopes he had brought. He and Father Elford began talking with the Central Americans individually. Most wanted the priests to make phone calls to relatives in El Salvador or in the States. Others needed help locating their papers. A few wanted to confess, and Corbett had to tell them he was a social worker with the church, not an ordained priest.

All the prisoners complained of hunger. Father Quiñones suspected that the prison cook, unhappy with having these extra mouths to feed, had dumped large amounts of chili pepper in their food. The Central Americans weren't accustomed to eating hot pepper, and when Father Quiñones first started visiting them in prison, he found many sick and the others half-starved. He brought medicine, soap, and toilet paper. He asked some of the ladies at his church to make more mildly spiced meals. María del Socorro Pardo de Aguilar, a housewife in her late fifties who volunteered at the Sanctuary of Guadalupe, went with Father Quiñones to the prison to help celebrate Mass and serve food. After her first few visits, the commandante began restricting the amount and kinds of food she could bring in. Corbett discovered in his conversations with inmates that the prison kitchen was run as a restaurant. Those Central Americans who couldn't afford to pay for their meals were given two dry corn tortillas a day, and, if they could scrounge a styrofoam cup from the restaurant's garbage, some soup.

Hard-boiled eggs were generally allowed, so Corbett began boiling three or four dozen every Wednesday. He also spent part of the day cutting pencils into 2-inch lengths, and he wrote out an information sheet, listing his and Manzo's phone numbers and explaining refugees' legal rights in the United States. He found there was a great demand for this kind of information. Most of the imprisoned Central Americans, having no place else to go, told him they were going to try to make it back up to the United States.

At that time, even Central Americans with valid tourist visas were being arrested and deported if caught in northern Mexico. Father Quiñones was able to win the release of some imprisoned people by bringing their passports to the head of immigration in Nogales. That official, Joaquín Figueroa, also began sending Salvadorans to Father Quiñones's church. But Figueroa's policy was the exception; when a new man was appointed in late '81, Father Quiñones lost his influence. Around that time, *San Diego Union* reporter Ricardo Chavira learned that an informal agreement existed between the U.S. and Mexican governments to deport Central Americans caught en route to the United States. Chavira also learned that U.S. immigration routinely turned over Central Americans caught at the gates, or within five miles of the border, to the Mexican authorities for deportation. Apparently this was done to save paperwork. The policy varied from region to region, as local officials in Mexico had a lot more autonomy than those in the United States, but generally, immigration officials on both sides of the border cooperated in the apprehension of nationals of other countries. "It's the neighborly thing to do," Chavira said.

Central Americans could always try to pay their way out. The shakedown at the Benjamin Hill checkpoint—on the road between Hermosillo and Nogales—ran about $100 in 1981, or so Corbett learned from people in jail. With the devaluation of the peso in '82, the bite came down to $20 or $30. Frequently, however, an immigration agent took a Central American's money and then arrested him anyway.

One of the favorite topics of conversation among the men in prison was what had tipped off the *migra* (immigration agents) to their nationality. Sometimes it had been their accent, but, more often than not, they'd been caught by the word *pisto*. In Mexican slang, *pisto* meant booze. To a Central American, it meant money. A Salvadoran may have known the difference, but when the immigration agent asked for it, he was so expecting to be approached for a bribe that his hand instinctively went to his pocket.

It took over an hour for Corbett and Father Elford to collect all the messages. They didn't go to the women's section this first day, but in the coming weeks, Corbett began making regular visits there as well. Sometimes he went with Socorro Aguilar, or a jailer would take him over after Aguilar and Father Quiñones had left. Women and young children (boys older than eight or nine were put with the men) stayed in the same area as the Mexican women. Corbett brought milk for the babies. It didn't take him as long to get the women's messages, since there were usually only half as many of them as of men.

Over the months, the church workers managed, little by little, to improve conditions in the women's section. Aguilar brought clothes and blankets collected at the church, and Father Quiñones convinced a few motels on the U.S. side to donate their stained mattresses. The men also needed bedding, but it was impossible to keep anything in their cell. Turnover was too great. The male prisoners were cleared out several times a week, and, when they were, the guards took what was left. In 1981, Corbett estimated, the Mexican government deported an average of eighty Salvadorans a week. Of these, he saw only a small fraction.

JUNE 26, 1981

The end of June marked the beginning of monsoon season in Tucson. Thunderstorms built up over the desert and came into town in the late afternoons, moving rapidly across the sky with great bolts of lightning and short, intense downpours. The storms rarely lasted longer than a few minutes. Sometimes the sun continued to shine while rain fell in a different part of town, and rainbows appeared through the billowy black clouds. Afterwards, the green-gray century plants and purple prickly pear stood out sharply against the dark sky and the air smelled of creosote bush, wet and resinous.

On such an afternoon, Corbett took Carlos and Chico and a third Salvadoran named Felix downtown to apply for political asylum. The three refugees had been staying in his apartment for several weeks. Since the day he met Carlos and Chico at Sacred Heart, Corbett had helped several other undocumented Salvadorans to enter the country. The only difference between them and people in the INS jails, as far as Corbett could tell, was that these Salvadorans did not have to be ransomed. The fact that the government considered them illegal aliens concerned him little. Corbett had talked with enough Salvadorans to become convinced that their lives were in danger if they were returned; he considered them political refugees, deserving of political asylum in the United States.

Whether they would get it was another matter. The year before, Congress had passed a law that was supposed to prevent political or foreign policy considerations from entering into the asylum process. Prior to that, the U.S. government had given preference to refugees from communist and Middle Eastern countries. The 1980 Refugee Act established the same criteria for asylum that the United Nations had established in 1951: "a well-founded fear of persecution on account of race, religion, nationality, membership in a particular social group, or political opinion." But the State Department continued to make recommendations on asylum cases that in almost every instance were accepted by the INS, and evidence was mounting that Salvadorans' asylum claims were not being judged by the same standard of proof as those from people fleeing countries at odds with the United States. Asylum approval rates for communist countries, and nations such as Libya and Iran, were between 50 and 80 percent in 1980 and '81. For Salvadorans, the rate was less than 1 percent. In 1983 and '84, the numbers of Salvadorans receiving asylum went up slightly, to between 2 and 3 percent. The INS then argued that, in terms of sheer numbers, it granted asylum to more Salvadorans than any other nationality except Iranians.

But there were many more Salvadorans who, if not deserving of political asylum, at least deserved temporary safe haven. That was the conclusion of an October 1981 study of INS procedures by the U.N. High Commissioner for Refugees. The UNHCR found that only one Salvadoran had been granted asylum in fiscal year 1981 (October 1980–September 1981) and that none had been allowed to stay in the country temporarily for humanitarian reasons. "It is fair to conclude that there is a systematic practice designed to secure the return of Salvadorans, irrespective of the merits of their asylum claims," the United Nations reported. An unpublished INS study written in 1982 concurred with the U.N. observations. "Certain nationalities appear to benefit from presumptive status while others do not," the study said. "For an El Salvadoran national to receive a favorable advisory opinion [from the State Department], he or she must have a 'classic textbook case.'" The author went on to compare this to the automatic granting of asylum to seven Polish crewmen who jumped ship in Alaska in December 1981, even though "all the applications, in the view of senior INS officials, were extremely weak." This study was later repudiated by INS general counsel Maurice Inman as "totally inaccurate from top to bottom." The INS continued to maintain that the asylum process was fair and impartial.

Much of the evidence that immigration courts were unfairly denying Salvadoran asylum claims did not surface until years later. In 1986, the General Accounting Office, Congress's investigative arm, did its own study of INS asylum procedures. The GAO found that in every case where the INS and the State Department disagreed on a Salvadoran's asylum claim, the INS changed its ruling to agree with the State Department. Republican Senator Arlen Specter of Pennsylvania said the GAO report indicated that "these decisions are not being made on the basis of merit, but on the basis of what is considered best for foreign policy." The Supreme Court added its voice to the criticism of the INS's handling of asylum claims in March 1987. The court decided in favor of a Nicaraguan who had been denied asylum by the government. By a 6–3 vote, the Court ruled that, under the law, she had to show only a "well-founded fear" of persecution, not a "clear probability," as the Reagan administration had required her to do. (Nicaraguan asylum applications had an approval rate almost as low as Salvadorans—7 percent in 1984. Since the U.S. government claimed that the Nicaraguan government was a gross violator of human rights, Corbett wondered why more Nicaraguans were not receiving asylum.) Many immigration lawyers believed the "clear probability" standard was impossibly high. They joked that refugees needed "a note from their dictator" to get asylum, but, in the case of Salvadoran, even that might not have been enough. Laura Dietrich, Deputy Assistant Secretary of State, said in *Atlantic* magazine in February 1987 that a note from a death squad would not be sufficient grounds to grant a Salvadoran asylum.

In late May 1981, Corbett had already had enough experience with the INS to assume that his three friends would be denied asylum in the end. He was helping them file primarily for the two or three years of freedom they'd have while their applications were on appeal. During that time, he hoped, the Salvadoran civil war would end.

The INS office was on the top floor of the eight-story federal building. Three rows of plastic chairs filled the tiny front room, pictures of government officials decorated the walls, and a clerk stood behind the counter taking applications. Corbett and the three Salvadorans took a number and sat down to wait.

When their turn came, Corbett went up and presented the asylum requests. The clerk looked them over.

"Just a minute please," she said, and took the papers to the back of the office. She was gone several minutes. Corbett knew right away something was wrong.

William Johnston, director of the Tucson INS office, came out. Johnston was in his mid-40s, balding and personable. He told Corbett and the Salvadorans to come with him downstairs to the investigations division. He needed to make an inquiry, he said. The Salvadorans, realizing they were being arrested, looked desperately at Corbett.

Corbett felt angry and betrayed. Johnston had changed the rules on him. Up until this point, he had been allowed to bring undocumented people in to apply for political asylum without risking their arrest. Manzo had represented several Salvadorans, such as Rubén, who had been released on their own recognizance after filing their asylum applications. Corbett believed this was the only way for a Salvadoran to get legal status without first being held captive at a high bond. Conversations with Father Quiñones and with Central Americans imprisoned in Nogales had convinced him that it was impossible to apply for asylum at the border. Anyone who tried was arrested, or turned over to the Mexican authorities.

Before this incident, Corbett had thought his role would be to help refugees avoid capture at the border, so that they might make it to Tucson or some other interior city to apply. Now there was no place for Salvadorans to request asylum without being taken prisoner. That meant the refugees would be better off staying underground. Corbett wondered if Johnston understood the consequences of what he was doing.

On the seventh floor, Johnston turned the Salvadorans over to the chief of the investigations division for processing. Then he told Corbett why he'd had them arrested. As Corbett recalled it, Johnston was quite specific that he was acting under orders from the State Department. Corbett said Johnston told him that all these Salvadorans applying for political asylum were beginning to embarrass the administration, which could not, for political reasons, call the government of El Salvador a gross violator of human rights. From now on, any Salvadoran who came in to apply for asylum would be arrested and sent to El Centro.

Johnston remembered it differently. These three Salvadorans were special cases. He'd had them arrested because he considered them likely to abscond if released. All had been deported previously, and one, as he recalled, had a criminal record from the Pacific Northwest. Johnston said he never got any State Department memos, and there was never any change in INS policy toward undocumented Salvadorans filing political asylum applications.

If that were true, Corbett wondered why Johnston did not say so at the time. Corbett would have kept bringing people in. As it was, Manzo's affirmative filing program stopped right there. Corbett told Johnston what was going to happen: The churches would have to start helping Salvadorans hide from the government. "We're not just going to abandon these people to their fate," he said.

Johnston seemed unconcerned about what the churches would or wouldn't do. Instead, he offered some advice on how to work with the legal system. Filing political asylum applications was a waste of time, he said. Johnston picked up one of the Salvadorans' applications and weighed it in his hand. "I can tell just by looking that it isn't going to pass," Corbett remembered his saying. "I haven't seen a Salvadoran application get approved yet."

Johnston suggested that Corbett try to get Extended Voluntary Departure for Salvadorans—a government designation that would allow them to stay here until hostilities ceased in their country. EVD, or its legal equivalent, could be granted by an act of Congress, or by the Attorney General at the request of the President. It had been given to Cubans in 1958, and at various times since to such nationalities as Poles, Afghans, Ethiopians, Iranians, and Vietnamese. President Carter granted it briefly to Nicaraguans following the 1979 Sandinista Revolution. The Reagan administration would never grant it to Salvadorans, Corbett knew, and Congress could take years to pass such a law. He was concerned about what might happen to these three refugees right now.

Corbett and Bill Johnston talked for almost an hour. They agreed that conditions in El Salvador were bad. Johnston even seemed to believe the refugees' claims of persecution, because he implied to

Corbett they ought to stay and fight instead of running away. "If they did things like that to my relatives, I'd shoot the bastards," were the words Corbett remembered. Johnston, who called himself a typical, loud-mouthed New Yorker, said that sounds like something he might have said.

At 5 o'clock, with the office closing, Corbett had to leave. The three Salvadorans were still being interviewed, in preparation for their being sent to El Centro. A computer printout had come back on one of them, showing only a prior deportation. "He was just in bad company," Johnston said later. Corbett drove straight to Manzo to tell them what had happened.

This event was a major turning point for Corbett. He felt that the INS had cut off the last legal avenue available for helping un-documented Salvadorans. Johnston thought Corbett exaggerated the importance of the arrests. "Let history record," Johnston said, "that one of the participants in this incident did not think it was any big deal."

EARLY JULY 1981

"The desert will lead you to your heart, where I will speak," read the inscription from Hosea on the chapel wall at Picture Rocks. Priests and religious groups came to the retreat, in the foothills of the Tucson mountains northwest of town, to pray or hold meetings. It was a peaceful setting, with an outdoor Way of the Cross that wound through a well-kept desert garden. Picture Rocks was named for rocks in a nearby ravine, painted with geometric and animal-shaped designs by Hohokam Indians in the thirteenth century. On the opposite hillside, a more recent Christian shrine stood among the saguaros.

The Tucson Ecumenical Council Task Force on Central America held its first major meeting in a small, book-lined conference room at Picture Rocks in early July. No more than ten or twelve people were present: Gary MacEoin, Tim Nonn, and Mike Smith from St. Mark's, Margo Cowan and Lupe Castillo from Manzo Council, John and Marianne Fife, Father Elford, and Jim Corbett were among them. Father Elford had invited Corbett, who was still an outsider to the TEC. Corbett and Fife met here for the first time. Barbara Elfbrandt, a Quaker lawyer who worked for the American

Friends Service Committee in Tucson, also attended. The AFSC was a Quaker social-service organization that had cared for war victims since 1917. The intended agenda of the meeting was the resettlement of Salvadoran refugees in Tucson.

Tim Nonn had found an old mansion he thought might be a perfect temporary shelter for bonded-out refugees. It had a lot of space, a pool, and, most importantly, it could be rented for $1 a month in exchange for general upkeep and repairs. The group planned to talk about the pros and cons of the house, but first they listened to a report from Margo Cowan and Lupe Castillo.

The two women had just gotten back from a trip to El Centro. They said the situation there was such that the refugees could not hang on very long. Inmates were made to stand outside all day, and there was not enough shade for everyone in the dirt-and-concrete prison yard. Some arrived very sick—even with bullet wounds or broken bones—and no doctor came to treat them. Skin infections were rampant. Prisoners weren't allowed to read anything except the Bible. (An INS guard later explained to Gary MacEoin that they would stuff the pages of other books down the toilet.) Everything about the place was designed to make the Salvadorans sign voluntary deportation orders.

Refugees had related to Cowan and Castillo how they were pressured into signing. They said they had been told they had no rights and no choices. They were led to believe that, if they didn't sign, they would have to stay in El Centro and then be deported anyway. Many never knew they could talk to a lawyer or file for asylum. Others were dissuaded from filing political asylum applications because INS guards told them the information they put down would be turned over to the Salvadoran government. As bad as it was, more than a hundred had refused to be voluntarily deported. They feared whatever awaited them in El Salvador more than they feared the INS.

Lawyers and refugee workers in the Los Angeles area were also aware of many instances in which the INS had denied Salvadorans their legal rights. In November 1981, the National Center for Immigrants' Rights filed suit on behalf of a Salvadoran named Crosby Wilfredo Orantes Hernández. The following May, the federal court issued a ruling in the Orantes-Hernández case that forbade the INS from deporting Salvadorans without fully informing them of their rights. U.S. District Court Judge David Kenyon went as far as to write in his opinion that "the INS engages in widespread illegality." Despite this decision, reports continued of INS officers using heavy-pressure tactics to extract voluntary departure agreements.

Cowan and Castillo's presentation of the situation at El Centro led the people at the meeting to rethink their priorities. They decided it was more important to bond out as many refugees as possible than to give ongoing care to a few. The resettlement-house idea was abandoned, and the group turned to organizing a mass bail-out of every Salvadoran at El Centro.

Corbett had already reached the conclusion that traditional social services weren't going to meet the needs of Central American refugees. The bond-out program was necessary for those facing deportation, and Corbett supported it. But the vast majority of Salvadorans were not in jail and needed to stay out. Corbett had already realized that their greatest need was to avoid capture, and he planned to help them do just that. He knew the organizations of TEC and Manzo weren't yet able to publicly help undocumented refugees. He did not even try what Quakers call "friendly persuasion" at Picture Rocks. He just said what he was going to do and why. Years before, in his goatwalking manuscript, Corbett had written something he termed the Quixote principle: "The social significance of a cultural breakthrough, as contrasted with a social movement, does not arise from its being done by vast masses of people but from its being done decisively by someone." Helping Salvadorans avoid capture was Corbett's latest cultural breakthrough.

The task force spent the next few weeks preparing for the mass bond-out. The TEC agreed to raise money and organize social services for the bonded-out refugees if Manzo handled the legal aspect. Tim Nonn assembled a volunteer force of fifty to go over to El Centro on July 10 and 11. Ken Kennon, the bearded pastor of Broadway Christian Church, was one of the people who went, saw conditions in El Centro, and was converted. He became a dedicated task-force member. Father Richard Sinner, a visiting priest from North Dakota, put up a quarter-of-a-million dollars' worth of his family land to provide the bulk of the collateral. Gary MacEoin and Ferner Nuhn, a member of the Claremont Friends Meeting, put up their houses, and Jim and Pat Corbett increased the lien on their trailer to $7,500 to make up the rest. Within the week, the task force had bonded out some 115 refugees—every Salvadoran in El Centro except for fifteen who were taken away and deported in the middle of the night. Corbett later described what happened in a letter to an INS official:

To break the refugees' morale and illustrate that we really couldn't change things, the camp commander ordered 15 of the refugees for whom we had filled out I-589s dragged out, screaming, crying, and clawing at the walls, to be deported to El Salvador. A few hours before it happened, I had completed the application for one of them, a middle-aged Salvadoran *campesino* who had worked all his life to build a herd of 15 Holsteins, which he'd had to abandon to save his life. I told him that, at least, he'd be safe now until things changed so he could go back, and that I could probably find him a job working cattle in Arizona. We talked cows for a while and parted laughing.

Carlos, Chico, Felix, Enrique Molina, and Alejandro Hernández were among those refugees given their freedom by the mass bond-out. Dudley's hitchhiker had long since been deported and was never seen by anyone in the Tucson group again. Two of the fifteen taken away in the night eventually made it back to the United States. They reported that one of the other deportees had been arrested by the National Guard when the plane landed in San Salvador.

The TEC task force was gaining new members every day, but internal conflicts also caused one of its founding members to drop out. Dave Sholin thought Margo Cowan was too autocratic and undependable and decided in mid-1981 not to work with Manzo. John Fife and Gary MacEoin agreed she was difficult, but, since Manzo was the only legal organization in town helping refugees, they felt they had to stick with her. Dave Sholin was also unconvinced that helping individual refugees was the best way to deal with a problem that could only be solved in Washington. He decided to put his efforts into starting a Tucson chapter of Clergy and Laity Concerned About Central America, a lobbying group that concentrated on changing public policy.

MID-AUGUST 1981

Corbett was going back and forth to Nogales every day now, sometimes twice, picking up refugees at Sacred Heart and taking them to the relative safety of Tucson. He put them in his apartment, or at the houses of a few friends around town who would let him. It was hard to find people willing to shelter undocumented refugees. Some backed out when they learned Corbett no longer had any intention of taking people to the INS.

Driving the back route to avoid the Peck Canyon roadblock, Corbett had ample time to think about what he was doing. The narrow, two-lane road wound through the grass-covered hills northeast of Nogales, down to the towns of Patagonia and Sonoita, and finally converged with the interstate 20 miles east of Tucson. It was a beautiful drive, especially in August, when the fat, blush bulbs of prickly pear were ripe and the barrel cactus bloomed yellow and orange by the side of the road. Corbett drove his green '61 Chevy truck. With refugees in the back, he looked like a local rancher and his field hands, and the Border Patrol never bothered him. Occasionally, he took the van he had loaned to Jim Dudley, but he didn't like to because it looked too much like a smuggler's van.

The fact that what he was doing was technically illegal bothered Corbett a lot less than it would most people. He had learned self-reliance early in life. "We just taught him to be honest and stand up for what he thought was right," Gladys Corbett said. Corbett's father, a lawyer, teacher, and Wyoming state legislator, also taught his son to be concerned with the rights of others. In the late '40s, when Corbett was in his early teens, his father talked about the Nuremberg trials at the family dinner table. "He would discuss the legal implications and insist international law applied to individuals as well as states," Corbett recalled.

Every summer during his childhood, Corbett and his parents and his sister, who was seven years older than he, moved to the Shoshone Indian Reservation or the Teton Mountains. They pitched a tent and lived off the land, catching trout and collecting wild plants. In the winter, Corbett remembered his family ate a lot of deer, moose, and elk meat, which was some of the most inexpensive food available in Casper, Wyoming. "We must have been poor in the '30s," Corbett said, "but I never had any sense of it. I never felt deprived."

The wide-open spaces of the West nurtured Corbett's independent nature. He spent a season sheepherding in Wyoming and found the solitary life to his liking. "Ranchers leave each other pretty much alone," he commented. Corbett went into the army in 1955, when his parents moved down to a ranch in the Huachuca Mountains, near Bisbee, Arizona. Less than three years later, Corbett got an early discharge to go help them fight a screw-worm epidemic. His commanding officer had wanted to get rid of him; Corbett said the captain once tried to have him courtmartialed for being a "demoralizing influence" but couldn't come up with a specific charge. "I've always been fairly good at being out of the way when they swat," he added. Corbett got assigned to an empty barracks and spent the rest of his enlistment reading works by Gandhi and other proponents of nonviolence.

Ranch life may have suited Corbett, but it didn't suit his first wife. She was a girl from Casper who had been attending Wellesley while Corbett was at Harvard. They had a daughter, with another daughter and a son soon to follow, when they moved on to Corbett's parents' ranch. The marriage lasted only three more years. In 1961, Mary Lynn took the children and went home to Casper.

Corbett reacted to his divorce with both relief and despair. He missed his kids terribly. He moved to Berkeley, California, studied a language called Bahasa Indonesia, and for a time spoke to almost no one. Then, a few months before his 29th birthday, he had an experience—although he was reluctant to call it that—which changed his life.

"My self-absorption reached a point of committing suicide," he said. "It liberated me in a way that resulted in an enormous, long, spiritual high that I have never really gotten off of. From what little I knew about Quakers, it made me decide I must be one." Corbett's spirituality was also strongly influenced by Buddhism, which taught (he said) that salvation comes with the realization that there is no soul to save. A letter Corbett wrote right after the Cuban Missile Crisis, published in the November 19, 1962, *Newsweek*, gave a picture of his thinking at the time:

"Each American who, whenever we are stripped of all other defenses of our interests and institutions, whimpers that we have no alternative but the impersonal mass murder of hundreds of millions of innocent people is already a murderer in his heart and a moral degenerate more abject and disgusting than a Hitler or a Stalin. There *is* an alternative. Every man who chooses to dedicate himself in all his acts to the love of his fellow man, even if he must perish in humiliation and agony, may be a seed from which peace will grow on earth."

Corbett said it would have been unthinkable for him to write a letter like that before his "conversion," but afterwards he felt instantly involved. He was living in Los Angeles, going to library school at the University of Southern California, and had just met Pat Collins. The two of them hit it off at once. Pat came from an upper-middle-class Republican family and had grown up riding horses near her home in the San Fernando Valley. She shared Corbett's love of the outdoors. "I only started asking him home to dinner," she said, "because he looked so hungry." Corbett was on a spiritual high and didn't need food. "It's a wonder I didn't starve," he said.

The Corbetts' first major disagreement came over the area of social action. Jim had decided, as do many Quakers, that he was not going to pay taxes. He didn't want to support the war machine in any form. "The Cuban Missile Crisis, where we just about blew the whole thing up right there, brought this home to me," he said. Pat objected. She thought her new husband would be hauled off to prison. "It was one of those things where she thought maybe people should do it, but she didn't want me to do it," Corbett said. The dispute was resolved when a friend asked Corbett how much he had made that year, and he discovered he hadn't earned enough to pay taxes anyway.

Corbett reached an understanding with Pat, but his now-active conscience continued to get him in trouble with other people. Two years later he was hired to teach philosophy and run the library at Cochise College, a junior college outside Douglas, Arizona. Corbett staved off school officials' attempts to remove *The Dictionary of American Slang* from the library, but that spring his conflict with them came to a head. The art teacher put up a show by two local artists in the library; one of the paintings depicted an American flag hanging in an outhouse with some chickens running off into a mushroom cloud. Corbett said the artist was making a negative comment about people who were afraid of nuclear war. Whatever it was, the governing board wanted it off the library wall. The art teacher took down the whole show in protest, and Corbett also protested. The school administration responded by refusing to renew his contract. Corbett's final letter to the governing board was published in that summer's issue of *Arizona Librarian*:

The fundamental issue creating the recent conflict has been the insistence that each person has certain inviolable rights of inquiry and expression

that should be protected from suppression. For the authoritarian personality—the man who wishes to exercise the greatest possible control over
the thoughts and actions of other people—such a position is intolerable,
immoral, and anarchistic. For the administrator who would rule rather than
govern, sanctuaries for individual choice and conscience appear as flaws in
organizational efficiency.

After assuring the board that he had no intention of filing suit
against them, Corbett concluded his letter:

Long before I anticipated working at Cochise College, I was fully aware that
conditions of this kind frequently arise and that loss of employment and pro-
longed periods of stress are inevitable occupational hazards of librarianship.
There is a Jewish folksong that proclaims, "Whoever treasures freedom,
like the swallow must learn to fly." Distressingly painful as they may be,
stress and confrontation provide the only atmosphere in which one is likely
to learn to fly. A man can suffer serious injury only from himself.

Distressing pain was very familiar to Corbett in the fall of 1965.
He could barely move around. The disease that would eventually
cripple him had first shown itself in August of '63, when Corbett
was taking his children on the bus back to their mother in Wyoming.
He had a high fever and a persistent headache, which doctors diag-
nosed as collagen disease—sort of a dissolving of the glue that holds
the cells together. They gave him six months to a year to live. Corbett had been working as a librarian at the University of Oregon and
studying Chinese. He decided there was no point in learning Chinese, and he and Pat moved back to Arizona. The symptoms went
away until the following year, when the trouble at Cochise College
surfaced. Then, the pain and swelling in his joints led doctors to
diagnose it as rheumatoid arthritis. Throughout the '60s and '70s,
Corbett would have flareups when he was under stress, but the crip-
pling and deformity didn't really come on until 1977, a year after his
father's death. Corbett said he never changed his life in any significant way as a result of his illness: "It's just made me more grateful
to be alive. It permits me to go on without being burnt out or worn
out. I think the Creation is pretty good, and I want to stick around
as long as I can."

Even the Vietnam War didn't change Corbett's basic optimism,
although he was amazed at what the United States would do to impose its will. He recalled reading an item in the Phoenix newspaper,

the *Arizona Republic*, in March 1965, which said Bihn Dihn province had been divided into quadrants and flyers instructed to bomb all the villages in each quadrant. "It was simply reported as ordinary news, with no indication there was anything surprising about the U.S. taking a whole province of South Vietnam and designating all the villages for bombing," Corbett said. "It came as quite a shock to me. I carried that clipping around for months afterwards."

Corbett started doing draft counseling for the American Friends Service Committee and the Fellowship of Reconciliation, an anti-war organization for religious pacifists. He sent information on conscientious objector status to every male student at Occidental, Loyola, and the University of California at L.A. After he and Pat went back to Arizona, he sent the same information to students at the University of Arizona, and he also worked on medical aid to Vietnam. This was Corbett's first experience with breaking the law for moral reasons; Quakers were sending medical supplies to North Vietnam in defiance of the Trading with the Enemy Act.

Despite his firm stance against the war, Corbett did not get involved in the radical chic that was sweeping college campuses in the '60s. The clenched-fist protests he saw as a librarian at Chico State College in California in 1968 lacked, in his view, a respect for truth. "The faculty members who were involved in protests had to identify themselves as an oppressed class of some kind, and, having lived much of my life cowboying and sheepherding, I didn't see too many oppressed people on the faculty of the California state system."

Corbett lasted at Chico State only a year. This time, his contract was not renewed because he protested the firing of a teacher who had been advisor to the Students for a Democratic Society on campus. The teacher didn't want to challenge it, but Corbett was concerned about everyone's freedom and tried to lodge a protest with the faculty senate. They refused to hear his protest and set up a secret committee to hear other librarians' comments on Corbett's ideas. Corbett responded by holding a one-man strike, and that was the end of his tenure at Chico.

Although running refugees around roadblocks was consistent with his history of taking direct action, Corbett said neither he nor Pat liked the idea. Both assumed it would be three months, at most, before he was caught. They didn't know what systems the INS used, and after reading about the Border Patrol's high-tech equipment, they decided the odds were against him. "You figure they have you no matter what," Corbett said. He never was caught, even though he made the trip from Nogales to Tucson hundreds of times over the next two years.

EARLY SEPTEMBER 1981

Southside Presbyterian Church was surrounded by a neighborhood of ramshackle houses and unkept, yellowing yards. Marianne Fife called it "the inner city." The barrio was wide open, with a view of the mountains like the rest of Tucson, but it was also dirt poor and only a few blocks from a freeway intersection. Southside's parsonage, behind a fence next to the church yard, had been a flophouse for a year before the Fifes moved in. Marianne had insisted that the Presbytery remodel it before she agreed to raise her children there.

Across the lot was a small, L-shaped church building. The schoolroom and offices, painted sky blue, extended to the side of the white, adobe chapel, and a carved, wooden cross hung above the door. Little vertical rows of silver bells decorated the porch supports. On the west side of the church was a playground, and shade trees, a young, armless saguaro, and sticklike ocotillos grew amid patches of dry grass in the yard.

The TEC task force began meeting at Southside in mid-July. They sat in the sanctuary, at the base of a huge, railroad-tie cross that took the place of an altar. A portable lectern, Fife's pulpit on Sundays, was pulled aside, and a blackboard set up. By September, the agenda for these meetings was being divided into three parts: TEC's social services, Manzo's legal services, and Corbett's evasion services—a name he thought up later for the border runs. "It wasn't called evasion services then," Fife said. "It was just called, 'go get 'em.'"

Fife agreed in principle that what Corbett was doing was right. He had even talked with Tim Nonn, Mike Smith, and Father Elford about clergy doing some of the driving. That way, if people were stopped, they could say they were doing church work. Talking, however, was as far as they'd gotten. Everyone already had a role to play. Elford was working with Manzo, Mike Smith was busy with the TEC, and the TEC wouldn't let Nonn do it. Fife was raising bond money through his church contacts and putting up refugees who'd been released from detention. There was a little apartment with a kitchen and bathroom in back of the church building, and any refugees who couldn't fit there slept on the floor of the sanctuary itself. For a while, Marianne Fife did all the shopping and cooking for the refugees, but that, on top of her job, soon became too much. The Southside women's association and other churches around town took on the task of supplying homemade dinners.

Concern for Marianne was probably the main reason why Fife was hesitant to help. The idea of her husband doing illegal things made her nervous, and at first she also had a real question in her mind as to whether John knew what he was talking about. "You hear such conflicting stories," she said, "and I thought, it can't be that bad. It was only after a lot of refugees came to our house, and just from talking with them, even with my very poor Spanish—we used to keep a little dictionary in the living room—I definitely got the idea. The stories were very similar and the fear was very real."

Although Marianne came to accept what the refugees were telling her, that did not lessen her fear of what might hapen to John if he were caught transporting or sheltering them. "It was the kind of thing I would have loved, if somebody else were doing it," she said. "I would have thought, 'Boy, what a fine person that is. I wish I had that kind of strength, and yes, of course it should be done.' But when it's your husband, and you know he might go to prison—it was just very frightening to me.

"People have different sets of priorities," Marianne explained. "My highest priority has always been my family—the kids and John. Anything I do, I weigh against how it affects them. Part of me was just screaming out that his priorities were such that he was willing to risk that for what he considered a higher priority. Which, of course, it is, but if I'm honest, it never would be for me. I guess that's kind of selfish. But that's who I am. I'd think about that, and think, well heck. He's obviously willing to—maybe he'll go to prison for a long time, and what does that do to our relationship, what does that do to the kids—I was angry about not only what would happen, but that he was willing to let it happen."

For a while, John Fife tried to balance the needs of the refugees with those of his wife. He reassured her that nothing bad was going to happen, and he continued his legal efforts to help refugees. But both of them knew he would eventually have to decide whether to join with Corbett or not. In early September, the moment of decision came.

After the task-force meeting broke up this particular Monday, Corbett walked with Fife out to the porch that ran along the side of the schoolroom. Fife lit a cigarette. The sky was a wash of pink and purple, the wispy clouds reflecting the last rays of light. For a moment, they stood and felt the warm air.

"John," Corbett began, "we're running out of places to stash people." He told Fife about the problems at his house. He had fifteen or twenty men living in the garage apartment, with its two small rooms and a bathroom. Pat was tired of fixing the constantly stopped-up plumbing. ("I really didn't mind them living there," Pat Corbett said, "except when they spat on the floor.") A few refugees were alcoholic or deeply troubled, and there'd been fights. Women couldn't stay in the same place as all those men, and Corbett had to find other places around town for them. He was having trouble remembering where he'd put everyone.

He also had another, more immediate reason for wanting to get the place emptied out. Corbett was leaving on a six-week field trip to Guatemala and southern Mexico, and he couldn't leave Pat to care for all the refugees. She had been the first to suggest that perhaps a church in town could take some of them in. It seemed to her there was a lot of space available, if Jim would just ask. Corbett did ask at a few churches and was refused. He'd decided to ask Fife.

"I'd like to bring people over to stay in the church," he said. "What do you think?"

Fife paused. "I don't know," he said. "I don't make the decisions around here. The church elders do."

Fife knew all Corbett's arguments for helping refugees avoid capture at the border. They'd talked about it before, and he'd read copies of Corbett's "Dear Friends" letters. They talked about it again. After thinking deeply, Corbett had come to the conclusion that churches must begin helping undocumented refugees. Too many lives were being lost, and too few Americans knew what was happening. The institutional church had power to influence public opinion that he, as a solitary Quaker, did not have. The points Corbett made to Fife this evening he made again five months later, in a statement to a National Council of Churches conference on immigration:

If the churches continue to ignore the Salvadorans' desperate need to avoid capture, the American public will continue to see the refugees, rather than their persecutors, as illegals.

Actively asserting the right to aid fugitives from terror means doing it—not just preaching at a government that is capturing and deporting them, not just urging legislation that might help future refugees. With people in our midst being hunted down and shipped back, denouncing the terror while ignoring the victims simply teaches the public how to live with atrocity.

Much more than the fate of the undocumented refugees depends on the religious community's participation and leadership in helping them avoid capture. If the right to aid fugitives from government-sponsored terror is not upheld in action by churches—regardless of the cost in terms of imprisoned clergy, punitive fines, and exclusion from government-financed programs—the loss of many other basic rights of conscience will certainly follow. No one who lives in this century can have missed that lesson.

Fife listened as Corbett went through the arguments. He was being asked to put the weight and reputation of his church behind a maverick Quaker and a group of illegals. He would have to examine his role as a husband and father, as a pastor of a congregation, and as a representative of the Presbyterian Church before he knew what to say. He told Corbett he'd let him know.

Fife pondered the question for several days. No matter how many objections he raised—the biggest one being the possibility that he was wrong—Fife could not escape his conviction that, if what the refugees said was true, it would be immoral not to protect them. And he did believe the refugees. So, ultimately, the decision was easy. Fife presented Corbett's request to a meeting of Southside's elders the following week. He explained the reasoning behind it, and when the elders asked for his recommendation, he told them he thought they should do it. That was good enough for them. By a 7 to zero vote, with two abstentions, the elders decided to house undocumented refugees in the church. Fife said the two abstainers also supported the decision but didn't want to be on record as having voted for it. One, Millie Paylock, said she feared a yes vote might jeopardize her pension from the Veteran's Administration. "I helped in legal ways, financially, and by working in the church office," she said.

A few weeks after the vote, Fife and others in the TEC task force started doing some of the driving as well. Marianne made John agree not to involve their sons in pickups at the border. She told him she couldn't be sure if the boys supported the work because they thought it was right or because of their devotion to him. She was still upset about the whole thing. It bothered her that people might think her husband was communist or subversive.

DECEMBER 5, 1981

In the early evening, in his hotel room in Malacatán, Corbett sat down to write a letter to Pat.

A few moments ago I was in the plaza, sitting and watching the evening promenade. There was a burst of pistol fire from the police station about 50 yards from me. Everyone scurried for cover, and businesses quickly shut their doors and turned off outside lights. I walked over to a place where a bus driver and passengers were peering from the corner of a building. There were lots of ideas about a guerrilla attack, but no one really knew why the police started shooting. I had to cross the plaza to get to the hotel, which faces the police station, but I figured it'd be best to get in. They had the door locked and the lights off but let me in when I knocked.

Soon the Guardia de la Hacienda (green uniforms), Guardia Nacional (blue uniforms), and secret police were in the plaza in force. The hotel owner said it wouldn't be good for me, a stranger in town, to go out. She also said if any shooting started, all those submachine guns would be very dangerous—they usually killed a lot of bystanders when they opened up— so I guess I'll spend the evening in the hotel.

It was only Corbett's second night in Guatemala. He had come here to make contact with priests, set up refugee relay routes, and to find out what the situation was like here for those deported from the Sonoran prison. In southern Mexico, where he'd spent nearly a month, he found many priests helping refugees. But in Guatemala, he found a fear-stricken tropical paradise. "The surrounding country is almost all pasture," he wrote Pat, "large holdings with well-bred Brahman, Gyr, Indo-Brazil, and *Bos indicus* × Brown Swiss. Planted areas are mostly 40 or more acres and in forage crops. It'd be quite good cow country, if people didn't have to suffer so much for it."

Guatemala had a history of colonial exploitation and rural poverty similar to El Salvador's. The country's military rulers had long used death squads to silence popular unrest, and in the early 1980s, thousands of Guatemalans suspected of being guerrilla sympathizers were killed. Corbett said in the letter that he'd counted six stories about eleven disappearances and three stories about seven recovered corpses in the morning paper. Another news story said guerrillas had torched four buses on the InterAmerican highway the night before. The rebels handed out leaflets to passengers while the buses burned.

"Nothing can be done, organizationally, to help the deportees," Corbett wrote. "The few priests left are the only ones who could be contacts, but they wouldn't last long if outsiders were in touch with them."

Across the border in Tapachula, a low-lying industrial city near Mexico's Pacific coast, Corbett had had more success. There the refugee population was too big to ignore. Busloads of deportees from the north, plus those coming over from Guatemala, had almost doubled Tapachula's population. One priest Corbett talked to estimated that thirty to forty thousand migrating Central Americans were in or around the city on any given day. Officially, Mexico maintained the U.S. government's policy of denying that the refugees were refugees: Corbett read in the *Diario del Sur* that the Procurator of Justice for the state of Chiapas had said "the majority of illegals have a criminal record and only come to commit crimes." Unofficially, the local government relied on the church to care for displaced people.

Corbett visited parish priests in the small towns surrounding Tapachula and found many of them housing Guatemalans and Salvadorans. He told the priests about the aid programs underway in Tucson and Nogales and arranged for a few of the priests to hold money for arriving deportees. Corbett had to be completely open —it was the only way to make contact—but he tried to phrase his questions in such a way that the priests would not have to reveal anything about their own activities.

One priest, a joyful charismatic named Padre Pedro, trusted Corbett immediately. He said his congregation was busy housing and feeding refugees, finding them jobs, and running them past checkpoints—many of the same things the Tucson group was doing. He invited Corbett out to a retreat in honor of the Virgin of Guadalupe, the patron saint of Mexico. Some three hundred Catholic charismatics were coming to pray and sing for a day. Amid the worship, Padre Pedro set aside an hour for Corbett to talk about refugees.

Corbett made what he thought was an inept speech. "Tucson is to the Mexican border what Tapachula is to the Guatemalan border," he said. "Many of the same situations are arising." He talked about the need for help all the way from Tapachula to Tucson. Then Padre Pedro had the participants break into small groups to decide what each could do. One group that lived in a village close to the roadblock at Huixtla volunteered to run people around it. Another raised pigs in their village, and they offered to give a piglet to the refugees imprisoned in Tapachula at Christmas. Some women from town said they could organize to make regular meals for the jailed refugees.

Corbett was fascinated that the question of whether the Mexican government considered certain activities illegal didn't even come up. Unlike Americans, the charismatics weren't troubled by conflicting loyalties; even wives of local politicians wanted to help. After the retreat, Corbett was invited out to a ranch, where he met the governor's brother.

Padre Pedro's use of the Christian base community model, as well as the overt influence of liberation theology on the Catholic Church in southern Mexico, contrasted sharply with the condition of the church in Guatemala. Corbett noted that religious repression in that country had driven the Catholic Church underground and had led to the rise of Evangelical Protestantism, which, rather than addressing the temporal concerns of the poor, concentrated on saving souls for the next world. Many conservative Catholics, disenchanted with their church's turn toward liberation theology, had become Evangelical Protestants. A tent-meeting near Corbett's hotel in Malacatán drew large crowds every night he was there.

Corbett spent several days in Tapachula before he took the bus to Talisman and Ciudad Hidalgo, the city's two border crossings with Guatemala. Refugees from up north were usually dumped on one of the bridges over the Suchiate River. Some were imprisoned in Tapachula again before being bused to El Salvador—often for several days without food, in order to persuade them not to return to Mexico. Other deportees were sent to the Guatemalan side, where, in 1981, soldiers generally allowed them in. Sometimes they were shaken down first. Other times they were told they had ten minutes to get out of the country.

At Ciudad Hidalgo, Corbett saw women with groceries wading across the Suchiate a couple hundred yards downstream, in full view of immigration officials on the bridge. Because cross-border traffic was good for the local economies, the guards allowed it to go unheeded. The Mexican *migra*, Corbett realized, was adept at spotting people who weren't from the area. He watched one young man come up on the bank into the grip of an immigration agent. He noted down to tell refugees that locals often wore Guatemalan straw hats and carried kerosene tins.

Corbett walked along the bank and met a woman who had lived in a house along the river for many years. She said, since the refugees started coming, bodies frequently floated by. The woman pointed to a shoe lying next to her and said, "This came off one they pulled out a day or two ago." Corbett saw it was a canvas slip-on, the kind made in El Salvador, which he already knew were dead giveaways to Mexican immigration.

"It must have been a Salvadoran," he said.

"Yes, it was."

Another afternoon, Corbett went down to Puerto Madero, on the Pacific coast about 20 kilometers from Tapachula. The large *zona de tolerencia* (red-light district) in that town was mostly a Central American ghetto. Some women Corbett talked with in the *zona* spoke unconvincingly about saving up for the bus trip north, but many had small children and clearly felt trapped. They couldn't figure out what Corbett wanted of them. He saw again the vulnerability of women refugees.

Throughout the trip, even when talking with refugees, Corbett posed as an arthritic rancher looking for a good retirement spot. Tourists were nonexistent in hot, humid Tapachula, and he needed an excuse to avoid attracting attention from the authorities. Everyone accepted his disguise when they saw his fingers. In Guatemala, he had to be even more careful. He left his diary and maroon Spanish Bible in Mexico, and the only thing he wrote during his five-day stay there was the letter to Pat.

The next morning, Corbett got the story on the shootout at the police station. "Two women from the cantina were picked up and put in jail," he wrote. "A drunk Green Guard, out of uniform, approached, maybe to join the 'fun.' Maybe he made a threatening gesture. In any case, he was armed and wasn't known by the men on guard, so he was shot dead."

Corbett went down to watch the refugee flow on the Talisman bridge that afternoon. He chatted with two Green Guards on duty.

"They say we can go into the cattle business cheap," he wrote Pat, "a solid $3 million *finca* [ranch] selling for only $1 million. (One was burned a few kilometers away a few weeks ago.) When I wondered about the risk of being killed, they said, in common with everyone else, 'There's no problem, if you don't get involved in politics.' The east is where they recommended for cattle ranching. 'There were guerrillas, but it's completely cleaned out now, empty and ready for cattle.'

"This area could produce enormous amounts of protein as a smallholder dairy belt," Corbett went on. "If Guatemala ever settles into popular rule, maybe we could come and help AI [artificially inseminate] the beef breeds towards Brown Swiss."

MID-DECEMBER 1981

A week or so after Corbett got back from Guatemala, the TEC task force held an emergency session in John Fife's living room. Margo Cowan had received a message from an INS lawyer in the hall outside a bond-reduction hearing, and, as Fife put it, the message was this: "We've been picking up aliens with Corbett's number in their pocket. We know what you're doing, and you'd better quit, or we're going to have your behinds."

No one was surprised. The group had decided a long time ago to be open to refugees, and that meant, sooner or later, discovery by the government. They'd kept the evasion services secret as long as they could, using pay phones and talking in codes no one could remember. Fife once puzzled over a telegram from Corbett for three hours before giving up. Now the cat-and-mouse with the Border Patrol was over, and the task force had to decide what to do next.

"We can do two things," Fife said. "We can keep on doing what we're doing, and wait for them to indict us. Or we can quit."

They went around the room. Corbett, Elford, Castillo—whether they did border work or not, everyone agreed it had to be done. Helping people avoid capture was preferable to having to bond them out. Fife was struggling to raise $2,500 a week to bail out the ten who had been in the longest. Gary MacEoin and a co-author, Nivita Riley, had begun researching their book *No Promised Land*, an examination of U.S. government treatment of Salvadoran and Haitian immigrants, and they'd confirmed many of the illegal and discriminatory practices that task-force members had observed. MacEoin had also found that the United States was ignoring pleas from the United Nations, Amnesty International (an England-based international human rights organization), and José Napoleón Duarte to stop deportations until hostilities ceased in El Salvador. The United States was also violating several international laws and treaties in its near-blanket denial of Salvadoran asylum applications. One of the immigration lawyers MacEoin interviewed, Mark Van Der Hout of Redwood City, California, commented that "the Salvadorans have the best cases for political asylum I've ever seen." Yet Gary MacEoin, and the rest of the TEC, had never encountered one Salvadoran who'd received it.

The task force finally reached the conclusion Corbett had come to months before: The legal route was doomed. Manzo had started advising refugees not to apply for asylum unless they were arrested. They risked arrest to apply, and, even if they weren't arrested, their chance of getting asylum was so small that entering the system voluntarily only served to accelerate their deportations.

The people in Fife's living room knew this situation could change if enough Americans cared about what was happening to Salvadoran, and now Guatemalan, refugees. So far, however, the public had shown very little interest in press conferences and prayer vigils. The media had done one story, on the El Centro bailout, and that was it. Congress was equally unresponsive. Ken Kennon said his visits to Senator Dennis DeConcini and Congressman Morris Udall had proved fruitless. (In late 1983, the legislature passed a "Sense of Congress" resolution saying that deportations should be stopped, but it had no force of law; apparently Congress was reluctant to challenge a popular president on a key aspect of his foreign policy.)

"We're going ahead, saving a few lives, but no one in the community gives a damn," Fife said.

There was one alternative to waiting for the inevitable arrest. They could go public. "Beat 'em to the punch," Fife said. They could claim the moral high ground, explain what they were doing, and maybe even rally support before the INS had them all branded as alien-smugglers. Everyone agreed it was a great idea. They discussed what form this public announcement might take.

Fife remembered a letter he had gotten in late October, from the Reverend John Wagner, director of the Lutheran Social Services of

Southern California. Wagner described a scene that had recently taken place in a downtown Los Angeles church. INS officers chased a man into the church and down the nave, until they finally caught him in an upstairs loft, where the man was handcuffed and led away. When church representatives lodged a complaint, they were told that, from now on, INS officers would not pursue anyone who had entered a church, hospital, or school.

"This order, in essence, is saying the church is a sanctuary, but it is not established as law," Wagner wrote. He urged pastors to consider reintroducing the concept of sanctuary, which up until the nineteenth century was a recognized function of the church. "Maybe the church as sanctuary will change some patterns of violence, of bureaucratic red tape, of waiting in prisons for hearings, of documentable people being precipitously sent away, of court decisions coming down so heavily against ethnic people, and of punishment that forgets the victims," he wrote.

Sanctuary. As the task force members talked, they realized that the church could serve as a platform, as well as protection, for the refugees. They had all been moved to get involved with refugees after meeting them and hearing their stories face-to-face, and they believed other people were likely to respond the same way. If the refugees' eyewitness accounts of atrocities in Guatemala and El Salvador were public, it would also make it more difficult for the U.S. government to deny that these things were happening.

Now the question was which church would do it. Everyone looked at Fife.

"Mine will," he said.

In January, at the annual congregational meeting, Fife put the issue up for a vote. He couldn't tell his parishoners what the consequences would be. He just explained the law regarding harboring illegal aliens and said it was unlikely the INS would prosecute an entire congregation. A four-hour discussion ensued. Marianne Fife recalled that two young black women spoke eloquently about churches sheltering their ancestors who had escaped from slavery. Someone else wondered why Southside was doing this on its own. Fife said he'd try to get other churches to join them.

The final vote, by secret ballot, was 59 to 2, with four abstentions. Prompted by Fife, Tim Nonn sent letters to congregations around the country that worked with refugees, asking them to join the sanctuary declaration. Representatives of five churches in the San Francisco Bay Area, some of which had also been sheltering refugees clandestinely, agreed to hold a similar ceremony at the University Lutheran Chapel in Berkeley; the First Unitarian Church in Los Angeles, Luther Place Memorial in Washington, D.C., and the Community Bible Church in Lawrence, Long Island, also decided to participate. The Episcopal Diocese of Ohio, the Unitarian Universalist Service Committee, the Arlington Street Church in Boston, and the Social Justice Commission of the Catholic Archdiocese of San Francisco sent endorsements. As the day for the event, the task force picked March 24—the second anniversary of Archbishop Romero's assassination.

Meanwhile, Gary MacEoin and Mike Smith were working to get the Tucson Ecumenical Council's endorsement of sanctuary. Dave Sholin, who as chief pastor at St. Mark's was still a strong voice on the TEC, didn't think sanctuary was an answer to the refugee problem. It was fine as a religious statement, he said, but it wouldn't change government policy and could lead to the arrest of refugees in the church.

Sholin was right in that no one could say for certain what the INS would do. It was possible they might show up in force at the declaration and arrest them all. In case that happened, the task force decided to have only one refugee stay at Southside for a while—one who knew and accepted the risk—and move the others to churches around town that had agreed to act as "quiet" sanctuaries.

MacEoin convinced Sholin that the refugees were in danger anyway, and a public declaration might actually help protect them from the INS. Task-force members also had to reassure the TEC, as well as Margo Cowan, that in spite of their frustration with the legal system, the bond-out program would continue. The TEC voted to endorse Southside's declaration, but it still didn't want Tim Nonn doing border runs.

MARCH 24, 1982

Southside's fluorescent-lit chapel overflowed with people, and, with the door open, the building glowed like a beacon in the spring night. Members of the congregation stood beside people of other faiths, races, and generations, who had come from all over Tucson, from different parts of the country, from Mexico, and El Salvador to join in the declaration of sanctuary. Even a plainclothes INS agent attended; the service this evening was truly ecumenical.

Earlier in the day, Fife, in a coat and tie, had held a press conference on Southside's front porch. Television cameras recorded him reading a letter that had been sent to Attorney General William French Smith, U.S. Attorney for Arizona A. Melvin McDonald, Bill Johnston, and Leon Ring, head of the Border Patrol in Tucson. "We ask that extended voluntary departure be granted to refugees and that current deportation proceedings against these victims be stopped," Fife read. "Until such time, we will not cease to extend the sanctuary of the church to undocumented people from Central America. Obedience to God requires this of us all."

Fife then introduced a refugee named Alfredo who would be living in the church. Alfredo, a stocky 30-year-old, sat with his arms folded and his leg jiggling nervously. He wore a cowboy hat and a bandana over his face, to prevent, Fife said, the Salvadoran military from discovering his identity and retaliating against his family back home. Until recently, Alfredo had worked for the government's agrarian reform program, an attempt to redistribute some land to the peasants, which had been brutally crushed by the army.

Gary MacEoin, Father Elford, Margo Cowan, and Jim Corbett made statements. "Today, in this church, human solidarity is out in the open, and oppression is in hiding, waiting for another time without witnesses," Corbett said.

The public declaration was already a success, in that it was well covered by both the local and national media, and it placed the government, at least temporarily, on the defensive. When asked by reporters several days prior to the announcement, Bill Johnston said he knew nothing about an underground railroad for Salvadorans headquartered at Southside Church. But documents that surfaced almost four years later proved that, not only was the INS aware of the sanctuary declaration, it had undercover agents at both the press conference and the prayer service. U.S. Border Patrol agent Thomas Martin, who wrote a memo to other agents after attending the press conference, referred to Alfredo as "the Frito Bandito" and to sanctuary supporters as "political misfits." Agent James Rayburn, of the Phoenix anti-smuggling unit, wrote in June 1983 that Tucson border patrolmen recognized Alfredo "as an alien they had placed on docket control earlier in the week." Corbett said that was impossible; he had brought Alfredo and his family into the country himself a few weeks before. Corbett and the Salvadorans were accompanied on their trip by Randy Udall, a reporter for the *Tucson Citizen* and son of Congressman Mo Udall.

Some two hundred people walked in a candlelight procession from the downtown federal building to Southside for the ecumenical service. As they gathered in the church, they knew an undercover agent was among them. It didn't matter. The spirit in the church was triumphant.

Fife, dressed in white robes with a Guatemalan, multicolored surplice draped over his shoulders, stood with several other pastors under the cross. The members of the congregation faced each other across the center aisle.

"On an occasion such as today," Fife began, "those of us who've worked long and hard tend to get a little self-righteous about what we've done and the contribution we might have made. God puts that all in perspective.

"Behind our cross are small crosses on the wall with a few names on them. They are the names of priests and pastors and religious women who have died in service of their God in El Salvador. Compared to Archbishop Romero, compared to those faithful priests and women, we have done nothing to deserve any credit at all."

The congregation recited the confession of sin together, and Fife spoke again.

"As part of the new community of faith, live with the marks of the kingdom in our lives and in our community. These are the marks: Blessed are the poor, blessed the gentle. Blessed those who mourn. Blessed those who hunger and thirst for what is right. Blessed the merciful. Blessed the pure in heart. Blessed the peacemakers. Blessed those who are persecuted in the cause of right. Indeed, blessed are you when people abuse you and persecute you and speak all kinds of evil against you for My sake. Rejoice and be glad for your reward will be great in heaven. That's how they persecuted the prophets before you.

"Let us, as God's forgiven people, vow more and more to live by grace and be God's faithful people as well. Amen." The people bowed their heads.

Father Elford, also in white, recited the beatitudes in Spanish. Then Joseph Weizenbaum, rabbi of Temple Emanu-El in Tucson, stepped to the lectern.

"I do not share with you a Christian faith—I am a Jew," he began. "What I share with you tonight is our common humanity. What I share with those who died—whose names are on this wall—is a common humanity. I share also the fact that my father was an undocumented alien. He did not enter in Arizona. He entered at Ellis Island. And I thank God each day that he was allowed to stay in this country, and that I can live here. And in that spirit I share with you the words from my tradition, and also from yours—the nineteenth chapter of the book of Leviticus:

"'If a stranger lives with you in your land, do not molest him. You must count him as one of your own countrymen. Love him as yourself, for you were once strangers yourself, in the land of Egypt. I am Yahweh your God.'"

The Spanish-speakers in the church sang a Salvadoran folk song, accompanied by guitars, and then the entire congregation joined in for a stirring rendition of "Through It All." Rose Johnson, Southside's pianist, led with her Gospel-singer vibrato, Marianne Fife and the rest of the choir raised their voices, and soon the sound filled the church, spilling out the door to the warm night.

Fife had invited G. Daniel Little, a Presbyterian minister from New York City, to give the sermon. Little, who was director of the General Assembly Mission Council in 1982, had just come from its conference on global perspectives. His sermon began with a plea to Americans to open their eyes to the hardship caused by the war in El Salvador. Then he said:

"We allow the power of law to cause further hardship and possible death, because great power works to create distance, which deceives us about the real effects of our power. Our basic problem is that we do not even consider the consequences. We do not even know that there are cruel effects for real people who are vulnerable. There comes a point where argument about consequences becomes a denial that consequences matter. We are part of a Biblical and prophetic tradition that confronts such deception by acknowledging it in ourselves, by calling for a new consciousness, and by ringing the alarm bell to wake up and pay attention to the unjust effects of our power.

"The alien and the refugee offer the moment when God's promise is clear," Little went on, "the moment when justice is tested. The moment when our own inner condition is revealed to us. It matters eternally how we treat the alien. It tells who we think we are. It tells who we think Jesus Christ is. It tells what we think God's promise is all about: 'Inasmuch as you did it to one of the least of these, you did it to me.' "

Rubén, the thin, bespectacled Salvadoran who had accompanied Corbett on his first visit to El Centro, spoke next. He thanked the congregation on behalf of the refugee community and announced in hesitant English that he and several other documented Salvadorans in Tucson and San Francisco were going on a hunger strike. The strike, he said, was to protest the treatment of their undocumented brothers and sisters.

The last song of the evening was "We Shall Overcome." The congregation stood and held hands, switching from English to Spanish as they sang.

> We shall overcome
> We shall overcome
> We shall overcome someday.
> *En mi corazón*
> *Yo sé muy bien*
> *Nosotros venceremos.*

Rabbi Weizenbaum gave a final prayer in Hebrew, and Father Elford offered a Spanish blessing. Fife spoke the final words in English.

"There's a word of our liturgy I like to repeat at times like this. It says, keep your anger but keep it without hatred. May the grace of our lord Jesus Christ, the love of God, and the fellowship of the Holy Spirit be with us all. Amen."

As the first church in the country to declare sanctuary, Southside Presbyterian took a big risk. No one knew how the government, and the general public, would react to this alliance between the church and the illegals. Southside had some support from institutional church structures, but there was still a great deal of hesitancy on the part of the orthodox church to accept the unorthodox methods espoused by Jim Corbett. Corbett and the others anticipated persecution, indifference, and scorn. They felt they were taking up the cross of Archbishop Romero, who had said, "We have to repeat continuously, although it is a voice crying in the desert: No to violence, Yes to peace."

INTO THE BREACH

The nationwide response to sanctuary was immediate and—compared to what TEC task-force members were expecting—overwhelming. In the weeks following the declaration, Southside received dozens of letters from churches, Quaker meetings, and synagogues across the country interested in declaring sanctuary. Not all were from what could be considered liberal or activist churches; letters came from mainstream, and even conservative, congregations. The people who wrote were deeply moved by the Salvadorans' plight, so much so it surprised Jim Corbett, who said he doubted he would have done anything had he not been directly confronted by refugees. Some congregations wanted to know how to find a refugee family, and what the penalties would be for sheltering one. Others offered to raise money or to provide legal or social services. Initially, many churches were concerned about the possibility of retaliation by the government. As months went by, and it became clear that the INS was not planning to arrest members of sanctuary-providing communities, churches that had been helping refugees in "legal" ways stepped over the line to join Southside's "illegal" declaration.

Corbett and the rest of the TEC task force were too occupied with day-to-day crises along the border to handle the requests for refugees and information. Thus, in August 1982, while on a trip with a Salvadoran family to the Wellington Avenue United Church of Christ in Chicago, Corbett asked the Chicago Religious Task Force on Central America to serve as national coordinator for a new underground railroad. Corbett envisioned a coast-to-coast network of volunteers willing to transport refugee families from the border to churches offering sanctuary in the interior.

The Chicago Religious Task Force, which consisted of a thirteen-member steering committee representing more than two dozen Chicago-area religious and humanitarian organizations, was initially reluctant. According to its newsletter *Basta!*, the Chicago task force was formed in January 1981 to "organize people of all religious persuasions to understand and challenge U.S. foreign policy towards Central America," and none of the Chicago task-force members had had any experience running a refugee-relay network. "Even forty hours of Jim Corbett border stories and desert theology did not break down their hesitancy," wrote Renny Golden and Michael McConnell, members of the Chicago task force, in their 1985 book *Sanctuary: The New Underground Railroad*. "But they promised him they would make inquiries nationwide and try to find an appropriate, more experienced collective. After a month with no results, they realized it was 'amateur hour' and they would have to shoulder the responsibility."

With the CRTFCA acting as coordinator, a loosely structured network of sanctuary churches grew up. By March 24, 1983, a year after Southside's declaration of sanctuary, some thirty religious communities were also "public sanctuary sites," and another two hundred, according to movement members, had either publicly endorsed the idea or were helping quietly. Chicago task force members wrote articles in religious magazines and published "how-to" booklets for congregations considering declaring sanctuary. Support from national, mainline church organizations was still not forthcoming, but many local church bodies had gone on record as having endorsed the idea. Archbishop Rembert G. Weakland of Milwaukee and Archbishop Raymond G. Hunthausen of Seattle were two prominent Roman Catholics who came forward to support sanctuary during its first year.

The primary reason for the growth of the movement was the ongoing carnage in El Salvador and Guatemala. Church and human rights groups estimated that, by 1983, the Salvadoran civil war had killed some 30,000 civilians and displaced another million, an estimated one-third to one-half of whom were living in the United States. The U.S. government had stepped up the war in El Salvador with almost half a billion dollars annually in military assistance; helicopter gunships bombed the twelve "free-fire zones" that Salvadoran Colonel Sigifredo Ochoa had designated in Chalatenango. Salvadoran Archbishop Arturo Rivera y Damas condemned the bombing of civilian areas; so did Americas Watch, a New York-based human-rights organization. In Guatemala, tens of thousands were killed by military terror during the early 1980s. An estimated 200,000 more had fled the country and were living in refugee camps on the Mexican border or in the United States. Only a tiny fraction of them had legal status. Mexican newspapers reported instances in which Guatemalan helicopters had crossed the border to attack the refugee camps. The ostensible purpose of doing this was to root out guerrillas in the refugee population.

The Reagan administration continued to maintain that Salvadorans and Guatemalans who fled here were, in the words of Peter Larrabee, director of El Centro in early 1981, "just peasants coming to the U.S. for a welfare card and a Cadillac." Immigration judges continued to deny all but 2 to 3 percent of Salvadoran and Guatemalan asylum requests. Those denied asylum, those who signed voluntary departure orders, and those forcibly deported were being returned to their countries at an average rate of five hundred a month in 1983. Senator Dennis DeConcini of Arizona and Representative Joe Moakley of Massachusetts introduced a bill in Congress to grant extended voluntary departure to Salvadorans, but it was stalled in committee. In the absense of any short- or long-term relief for Central American refugees, sanctuary moved to fill the gap.

Another major reason for the rapid spread of sanctuary was the sympathetic media attention it received. Sanctuary workers in all parts of the country appeared on local television and newspapers, and Jim Corbett and John Fife received a great deal of national print and network coverage. In August 1982, a long article on Corbett appeared in *People* magazine, and he and Pat were featured on a 60 Minutes segment that fall. Dozens of major newspapers, including the *Washington Post*, the *Chicago Tribune*, and the *Christian Science Monitor* joined the religious press in chronicling the activities of the underground railroad. Corbett took reporters on treks across the border with refugees, patiently explaining his theory and method as they hid on their bellies in drainage ditches beside dusty Mexican highways.

"The press has an unending appetite for border crossings," Corbett commented, fully aware that his relationship with the media was mutually beneficial. "We find ourselves going to extremes to awaken Americans because the crucifixion of entire peoples is not particularly newsworthy while it's happening," he told a group in Austin, Texas, in October 1982. "One massacre is very much like another, and an ongoing slaughter soon ceases to be news. In my case, the attempt to bring the situation to public attention has involved the absurdity of smuggling refugees under a steadily increasing glare of publicity. The media are not interested in the indigenous martyrs of Central America, but they are fascinated with the willingness of U.S. citizens to go to some slight risk in order to help refugees evade capture."

A final reason for sanctuary's acceptance was that it seemed to be working. Because the government maintained its unwritten policy of not going into churches to arrest people, the refugees were, in fact, somewhat protected by a public declaration. For church people, there appeared to be little risk. "The Border Patrol van used to come by here all the time," Fife told an interviewer. "We haven't seen one since the day we declared sanctuary." Local officials answered reporters' frequent questions by implying they had bigger fish to fry. "The church groups were baiting us to overreact," Leon Ring, head of the Border Patrol in Tucson, told the *Arizona Daily Star* in December 1982. "Therefore, we have been very low-key. Certain arrests could have taken place, but we felt the government would end up looking ridiculous, especially as far as going into church property —anything where the ethics involved would be questioned."

INS spokesmen in Washington dismissed sanctuary as a political statement by groups opposed to President Reagan's Central American policy. "This is just a political thing dreamed up by the churches to get publicity—a game to pressure the government to allow Salvadorans to stay here," Bill Joyce, assistant general counsel to the INS, told the *Christian Science Monitor* in August 1982. "If we thought it was a significant problem, then maybe we'd look at it. But there are plenty of illegal aliens out there." Throughout 1982 and '83, the government put on a public face of wait-and-see, apparently hoping that sanctuary would die out on its own. Privately, as trial testimony would show, the government was keeping close tabs on the movement's progress.

Despite their official hands-off policy, INS spokesmen made it clear that they would not hesitate to prosecute any sanctuary workers stopped on the road. Rumor had it that Jim Corbett's picture was posted in Border Patrol offices all over southern Arizona, and an INS official warned in the *Washington Post* that "there are Border Patrol officers who would dearly love to catch him." By mid-'83, Corbett felt he was too well-known to go to Nogales, and he turned over the weekly prison visits to Philip Conger, a 25-year-old son of Methodist missionaries who had replaced Tim Nonn as TEC task-force project director shortly after Southside declared sanctuary. The Corbetts also stopped housing refugees at their apartment. In 1983 and '84, Jim concentrated more on writing and traveling, speaking to different groups around the country, and helping expand the sanctuary network. Others in Tucson (including Phil Conger, who'd been given permission by the TEC) took up border-breaking. Corbett continued to attend meetings, and he kept his hand in with an occasional "country crossing" (bringing refugees across a remote stretch of border, where the danger of capture was minimal), usually accompanied by a reporter and photographer. He took other sanctuary workers to southern Mexico and showed them the disguises and subterfuges he employed to get people past checkpoints. Pat Corbett worried about her now-notorious husband during these trips. If he were caught with refugees in Mexico, there would be no due process of law to protect him.

The celebrity of some of its members also led to changes in the structure of the TEC task force on Central America. In 1981, before he went to southern Mexico and Guatemala for the first time, Corbett started an organization called the Tucson refugee support group to do some of the border work he had been doing alone. The Trsg (Corbett prefered the lowercase letters, so as not to compete with other organizations) had many members in common with the TEC task force, but it focused completely on evasion services. The task force began to take on a more public function. Some founding members left the group: Dave Sholin retired as pastor of St. Mark's, Tim Nonn went to seminary in San Francisco, and Margo Cowan left for law school in Washington, D.C. Manzo Area Council was incorporated into the TEC and renamed Tucson Ecumenical Council Legal Aid. Lupe Castillo continued to work for TECLA. A Central American support organization, Techo (meaning roof), was founded in Tucson. Father Elford continued to hold weekly prayer vigils in front of the federal building, and Gary MacEoin kept writing and researching out of his office at St. Mark's. New volunteers arrived from all over the country to take up the border work, while dozens of reporters, authors, and filmmakers descended on Corbett and Fife requesting interviews and book, movie, and television rights.

Increased attention in 1983 also led the TEC task force to refine its definition of sanctuary. At first, they had believed that what they were doing was civil disobedience, in the tradition of Henry David Thoreau and Dr. Martin Luther King, Jr. But conversations with Gary MacEoin, Ira Gollobin of Church World Service, and other lawyers familiar with international law convinced them that they were, in fact, acting in accordance with treaties that the United States had signed and was bound to uphold. The 1948 Geneva Convention forbade signatories from forcibly deporting refugees back to a war zone. Even if, as the U.S. government claimed, the majority of Salvadorans and Guatemalans in this country were not *personally* singled out for persecution and were therefore not eligible for asylum under the 1980 Act, they *were* refugees from a war zone and thus entitled to remain here temporarily. It made no difference that they entered the country illegally or that they came through a third country to get here, or even that they may have "voluntarily" agreed to be deported. And since these refugees had a right to be here, it was also not a crime to help them enter the country or hide from the immigration service. This discovery caused the TEC task force to change its concept of sanctuary. It was not civil disobedience; it was civil initiative. Sanctuary workers were following laws that the government was breaking. (Thoreau had also formulated this position regarding Americans who disobeyed the Fugitive Slave Law: "They are the lovers of law and order who uphold the law when the government breaks it.") TEC members tried valiantly to explain the difference to reporters, but the perception that sanctuary was illegal remained widespread.

Sanctuary's growth from one man's cultural breakthrough to a nationwide social movement was not without problems. In 1983, the different styles of the Tucson and Chicago task forces that had initially complemented each other began to conflict. The Chicago group felt that Tucson's insistence that sanctuary was legal was a tactical switch designed to bring in supporters who were afraid of breaking the law. Chicago wanted the sanctuary movement to state

its willingness to break the law, to challenge the U.S. government's
Central America policy, and, according to the July 1984 *Basta!*,
"generate a mass effective domestic resistance movement within the
U.S." Their goal was to stop the killing in Central America as soon
as possible, and the best way to do that, in Chicago's view, was
for the sanctuary movement to stage marches, demonstrations, cara-
vans, and other public actions. They maintained that the TEC task
force's Quaker style of just allowing the movement to happen would
never bring about the desired changes. "We don't want to develop
the perfect sanctuary model," Chicago task-force member Don Dale
told the *Los Angeles Times* in February 1983. "We want to stop U.S.
intervention in Central America."

One aspect of the disagreement between Tucson and Chicago
centered on the use of the railroad. Chicago wanted to restrict the relay network to only those refugees going into public sanctuary. This
conflicted with the practice of the TEC task force and the Tucson
refugee support group, which had found that the number of refugees
willing to go into public sanctuary was small, perhaps 10 percent of
the total who came through Tucson. They did not feel it was right to
exclude from aid those who wanted to live quietly with their families, or just disappear into a Salvadoran community in a large city.
Many severely traumatized refugees were unwilling or unable to tell
their stories over and over again. Chicago task-force members said
they were only trying to prevent *borrachos* (drunks) and other un-
desirables from using the railroad, but they yielded when they saw
how strongly the people in Tucson felt about the issue.

The question of whether the movement should help right-wing
refugees, who did not necessarily support the goal of ending U.S.
intervention, was more difficult. In 1983, the TEC and Trsg adopted
a set of screening procedures that was based on the guidelines established by the U.N. High Commissioner for Refugees. Political ideol-
ogy was not a consideration; the determining factor was the Tucson
group's assessment of the level of danger faced by a refugee if returned. "High-risk" refugees, those most deserving of aid, had a
letter of recognition from the UNHCR, documents from reputable
human-rights organizations, or showed torture marks. "Medium-
risk" were members of targeted groups—union leaders, catechists,
army deserters, released political prisoners, and, in certain cases,
doctors, students, and young men in contested areas. The "low-risk"

refugees were everyone else fleeing *la situación*, the refugees from
what the Geneva Convention on War and War Victims had defined
as "either an armed conflict or a government that is a gross violator
of human rights." The Tucson sanctuary groups discussed each case
individually and had to agree unanimously to render aid before any
was given. If refugees could stay in Mexico, or get asylum in Canada
(which was accepting many Salvadorans and Guatemalans refused
asylum by the United States), they were encouraged to do so. The
Tucson groups also maintained a strict policy against working with
coyotes. They agreed it was important for sanctuary to distance itself
from those who profited from refugees.

By discounting a refugee's political sympathies in determining
whether to render aid, the Tucson groups were opening themselves
up, theoretically at least, to army deserters, right-wing Salvadorans, and Nicaraguans fleeing conscription into the Sandinista army
(although not many of these came through Arizona). The idea of
sheltering potential death-squad members was repellant to many,
and Corbett had a little difficulty prevailing with the argument that
restricting sanctuary to people with the "correct" political orienta-
tion would turn it into a mirror-image of the government's partisan
treatment of refugees. "We have to try to maintain the integrity of
the process," Corbett said. "We have to obey the law, to help people who are high-risk refugees—not to become indiscriminate in our
efforts to be heard." After considerable discussion, the members of
the TEC task force agreed to send a statement to the Chicago task
force that read, "We provide sanctuary to the persecuted, regardless
of the political origins of their persecution or of their usefulness in
promoting preconceived purposes."

Part of this position was Corbett's belief that it was important to
keep working with the INS. He wrote letters and met with government officials, trying to get them to accept asylum applications from
undocumented people and to allow refugees in transit to Canada
to stay in the United States temporarily. His efforts did not initially
lead to any changes in policy. But, he said, "we very much need to
preserve what has been developed. A very good structure of human
rights and equality under the law has developed over the centuries,
and we are the beneficiaries of that. I disagree with those who think
the whole system has to topple. In that sense, I'm a conservative."

The Chicago Religious Task Force disagreed with Corbett's formulation of sanctuary as a nonpartisan defender of human rights. Chicago wanted to focus its energy on anti-intervention activities, and its members felt that Corbett was undercutting their role by insisting that sanctuary be limited to evasion and legal services. "You reduce the multidimensional process of solidarity to apolitical humanitarian band-aids rather than expanding it to include all that comes from choosing the side of the oppressed. . . . ," the task force wrote in a letter to Corbett on February 10, 1984. They also argued that Corbett was being divisive, by separating the "good church" (that which helps refugees) from the "bad church" (that which has expressly stated political goals). "Some call the sending of medicine to a war-torn country 'humanitarian' but then label efforts to stop the flow of weapons that do the killing in the first place 'political,' " the Chicago task force wrote. "To separate the religious from the political in this fashion is to create a false dichotomy. . . . During the rise of the Third Reich, Dietrich Bonhoeffer said that the church must of course bind up the victims being crushed beneath the wheel, but there comes a time when the church must be the stick put in the spokes to stop the wheel from crushing the people."

Corbett said he understood the rage and frustration that the Chicago task-force members felt, and he conceded that priorities might be different there than on the border, where a constant stream of refugees kept everyone busy just performing direct services. But he also felt that to establish sanctuary on a platform, no matter how worthy, would reduce it to the level of another political pressure group. "The conviction that we can do no more for the persecuted than petition their persecutor deadens congregations even more than does their fear of becoming illegals," Corbett wrote. In his letters and speeches in 1983 and '84, he began to describe sanctuary as a spiritual place, beyond the coercive, power-serving world. In September 1984, the Institute for Policy Studies gave its annual Letelier-Moffitt Memorial Human Rights Award to the sanctuary movement. Pat Corbett read the acceptance speech, in which she explained her husband's view:

Sanctuary is independent of traditional political activism because the covenant people is formed by creative service rather than competitive struggle. As a result, the movement is politically as well as religiously ecumenical; it bridges and transmutes the partisan separations formed by our creedal, cultural, and factional differences. Sanctuary has germinated, taken root,

Jim Corbett in front of the Friends meeting house in downtown Tucson. Although a Quaker in belief and practice for more than two decades, he did not formally join the Pima Monthly Meeting until 1983. (Photograph by Harvey Finkle)

Pastor John Fife. He led his small Tucson congregation into uncharted territory when he urged it to declare sanctuary in 1982. (Photograph by Sterling Vinson)

Participants in the March 24, 1982, sanctuary declaration. *Seated, left to right:* Father Ricardo Elford, Alfredo, John Fife, Gary MacEoin, Mario Marín, Tucson Ecumenical Council President Joanne Welter, and Jim Corbett. *Standing, left to right:* The Reverend David Sholin, refugees Hector and José, Mike Smith, and Ken Kennon. The signs read, "INS: Don't profane the sanctuary," and "This is the sanctuary of God for the oppressed of Central America." (*Tucson Citizen* photograph by Peter Weinberger)

Refugees attempting to cross the Suchiate River between Guatemala and Mexico in 1984. (*Sacramento Bee* photograph by Michael Williamson)

Corbett helping Juana Alvarez over the fence into the United States. The government was unable to use this photograph as evidence because the photographer, Ron Medvescek, refused to testify that he had taken the picture at the border. (*Arizona Daily Star* photograph by Ron Medvescek)

Prosecutor Donald Reno, who worked as a nightclub owner and concert promoter before joining the U.S. Attorney's office in 1984. (Photograph by Ricardo Valdivieso)

Government informant Jesús Cruz in one of the few known photographs of him. (Photograph by Ricardo Valdivieso)

The eleven defendants. From left to right: *front row,* Sister Darlene Nicgorski, Socorro Aguilar, Nena MacDonald; *second row,* Peggy Hutchison, Wendy LeWin, Mary K. Espinoza; *third row,* Father Tony Clark, Jim Corbett, Phil Willis-Conger; *fourth row,* John Fife and Father Ramón Quiñones. (Photograph by Ricardo Valdivieso)

Jim Corbett, his mother Gladys, and wife Pat, chatting with Socorro Aguilar on their way to court. (Photograph by Harvey Finkle)

U.S. District Judge Earl Carroll leaving the court for lunch.

Marianne Fife after the verdicts. "No one could believe it," she said.

and flourished in Tucson, not because we are converting to more radical political beliefs, but because faith communities are accepting the yoke of the Kingdom. . . .

Not all factions in the sanctuary movement agreed that the Kingdom had come. Renny Golden, poet, journalist, and member of the Chicago task force said, "It's simply not true that sanctuary transcends the political. We have a responsibility not to take what could be the most beautiful position—what could be possible in other worlds—but to do what is historically possible."

This dispute, rooted in different theological and philosophical positions, took place on a literal level between Tucson and Chicago throughout 1984. The two groups disagreed over how the movement should be organized; Corbett and Fife wanted a horizontal network of sanctuary congregations, with no one person or organization directing the movement, while Chicago wanted an elected board of representatives to set policy and goals for sanctuary. They disagreed over whether sanctuary was civil disobedience or civil initiative. They disagreed over who was playing into the government's hands more: Chicago, by explicitly stating political goals, or Tucson, by trying to separate itself from those statements. The debate, which took place in letters, over the telephone, at meetings, and in *Basta!*, did not prevent the spread of sanctuary. By mid-year, more than one hundred and fifty congregations had declared. It did hamper communication between these congregations, however. The dispute reached a low point in October, when Chicago refused to release its mailing list of all the sanctuary sites to Tucson, which was planning a nationwide symposium on sanctuary for January 1985. Corbett responded to this refusal with a ten-page, single-spaced letter, published in the January 1985 *Basta!*, which said he did not wish to get involved in an organizational struggle and was resigning from the board of the TEC task force. Corbett also announced that he was withdrawing from a public role on organizational issues within the movement. It was a short-lived retirement.

Despite these conflicts, the sanctuary movement gained widespread acceptance in 1984. By the end of the year, every major Protestant denomination (with the exception of the National Association of Evangelicals) had endorsed the movement, and, although the nation's Catholic bishops refrained from making any statement as a group, individual bishops continued to lend their support. The Chicago task force estimated there were more than 70,000 sanctuary-movement members in the United States. Among them were people from all walks of life, from all shades of the political spectrum, from all races, creeds, colors, and faiths. Its broad support led INS officials, for the first time in their public statements, to respond seriously to charges made by movement members. The government defended its policies, saying that (1) Central Americans fleeing political persecution could stay in Mexico, (2) that the State Department conducted a study in mid-1984 and found not one of five hundred deportees had suffered persecution in El Salvador, and (3) that El Salvador was now a democracy and its government's human-rights violations were a thing of the past.

In a March 1985 debate with Laura Dietrich, head of the State Department's political asylum office, Jim Corbett countered these claims. "Mexico has not signed the U.N. Refugee Protocol, and there is no way to prevent the summary deportation of Salvadorans and Guatemalans who are caught in Mexico, no matter how strong their asylum claim happens to be," Corbett said. He pointed out that, as illegals, few refugees made it through Mexico without suffering some form of extortion. "But," Corbett added, "this is actually a false issue. Nothing in the law permits the U.S. government to return refugees to persecution in their homelands if they have resided in or crossed other countries, nor does the fact that refugees have economic needs alter their status as refugees."

Concerning the survey of deportees, Corbett gave the following response:

The State Department started with the names of 482 deportees. One hundred and eighty-eight of the names and addresses turned out to be fictitious or incomplete. Seventy-three could not be reached because they lived in areas of armed conflict where it was too dangerous for the investigators to go. In other words, information was gathered on a select sampling of 221, less than half of the purported sampling. Everyone who deals with Salvadoran refugees knows that refugees who have reason to fear persecution give false names when apprehended, which means the most likely victims were deleted from the original sample. The admission that 73 of those deleted were in areas of armed conflict too dangerous for the investigators to visit constitutes nothing less than a confession that the Geneva Convention rights of these deportees were violated by the U.S. government.

A letter to one of these was returned with the notation "deceased," but was undifferentiated in the survey's tabulation. Only 121 of the named deportees were interviewed, one of whom said he had never been in the United States. Family members or friends were interviewed in the remaining cases. Because refugees who fear return often use the name of someone they know who would clear a routine check, a number of the 221 persons named in the select sampling were also probably surrogates rather than deportees.

Salvadorans were hired to interview those named in the select sampling, by phone in many cases, asking whether they suffered persecution upon their return. Now, what do you suppose a Salvadoran is going to say if an investigator calls or comes to a residence and asks whether that person or an immediate relative has suffered persecution? One thing is sure: Many of the persons named are now long-gone after having learned that an investigator came looking for them. As with most of the State Department's recent publications about Central America, this survey is a calculated fraud.

The one person reported to have been murdered is listed as "mistakenly killed in guerrilla conflict," which reminds me of an inscription vigilantes once put on a gravestone in Tombstone's boothill, "hung by mistake." Like the vigilantes, the State Department has a peculiarly inclusive understanding of what is accidental. When asked to provide cases of deportees who had suffered persecution, the American Civil Liberties Union [in a 1984 study] gave the State Department a list of more than 100, but the State Department then declared the ACLU cases "accidental" and continues to maintain that there has been no documentation whatever of deportees' suffering persecution upon their return. The ACLU cases were discovered by matching a list of names and addresses given by deportees with lists of the names of Salvadorans documented by human-rights organizations to have been murdered, disappeared, tortured, or arbitrarily imprisoned. On the advice of church and human-rights organizations, the ACLU did not field investigations of the kind done by the State Department because such investigations terrify and jeopardize deportees and their families. Consequently, the documented cases cannot be considered, as the State Department has claimed, to represent the total number of those on the deportee lists who actually suffered persecution after being returned.

The third contention Corbett responded to was that El Salvador was now a democracy. This was a frequent government claim, because in order to keep U.S. aid flowing to the Salvadoran government, the administration had to certify to Congress twice a year that human-rights abuses in El Salvador were declining. Corbett said:

True, if El Salvador were a genuine democracy, then the Salvadoran military would not murder and torture citizens. Which just goes to show that elections can be as much a charade under the rule of military terrorism as they are in communist countries. For tactical reasons, the death squads are killing more discriminately now than they did in 1981, but there has been no structural change that would empower the nominally civilian government either to disband them or to hold their members accountable. El Salvador continues to rank with Guatemala [in United Nations, Amnesty International, Americas Watch, and other international and humanitarian groups' studies] among the very worst of the world's gross violators of human rights.

The ongoing gross violation of Salvadorans' and Guatemalans' human rights has been better documented than has been the case with other first-asylum refugees to have arrived in the United States during recent decades. The State Department's insistence that there is no evidence that they are actually refugees is in a class with the tobacco lobby's insistence that there is no truly scientific evidence that smoking is unhealthy. Using the U.N. Refugee Protocol's narrow definition, the U.N. High Commissioner for Refugees' office in Mexico City has found that more than half of all Salvadorans it has interviewed do, in fact, have a "well-founded fear of being persecuted for reasons of race, religion, nationality, membership in a particular social group, or political opinion."

The same year, 1984, also saw the first arrests of sanctuary movement members. In February, Stacey Lynn Merkt, Sister Diane Muhlenkamp, and Jack Fischer, a reporter for the *Dallas Times-Herald*, were arrested with three Salvadorans while driving outside McAllen, Texas. Merkt and Muhlenkamp worked at Casa Oscar Romero, a hospitality house for Central American refugees primarily funded by the Roman Catholic Diocese of Brownsville, Texas. They were both charged with four counts relating to the transportation of undocumented aliens; Merkt pleaded not guilty, and Muhlenkamp, apparently intimidated, agreed to testify against Merkt in exchange for not having to go on trial herself. The reporter was not charged.

Represented by Daniel Sheehan, a nationally known lawyer who had worked on the Pentagon Papers case, Merkt went on trial in May. The jury heard testimony from the INS District Director in Harlingen (the district where the arrests took place) that he had never granted asylum to any Salvadoran and that he, in fact, arrested undocumented asylum applicants, but Judge Filemon Vela instructed the jury not to consider any defense theories based on this evidence. "Indeed," wrote lawyer Ignatius Bau in *This Ground Is Holy*, "Judge Vela specifically instructed the jury to find that Merkt still violated the law even if she sought to help refugees apply for asylum elsewhere, such as San Antonio, the location of the next nearest INS district office." The all-Hispanic jury deliberated for three and a half days before finding Merkt guilty of three felonies. Judge Vela sentenced her to two years' probation and a ninety-day suspended sentence. Sheehan appealed the decision to the Fifth Circuit.

Less than a month after Merkt's arrest, on March 7, Phil Conger, the project director of the TEC task force, and Katherine Flaherty, a volunteer at Southside, were arrested with four Salvadorans in their station wagon on Highway 82 outside Nogales, Arizona. Conger was carrying a briefcase full of papers, many written by Jim Corbett, that described refugee routes through Mexico and contained information on the sanctuary network in the United States. Flaherty was not charged, and the four counts brought against Conger were dropped, when the judge ruled that the Border Patrol had had no probable cause to stop the car. But, according to Corbett, the papers seized in the arrest proved instrumental in the government's decision to launch an undercover investigation of the activities of the TEC Task Force on Central America.

In late March and early April, a stout, middle-aged Mexican named Jesús Cruz began showing up around Southside, saying he sympathized with the movement and wanted to help. Members of the TEC task force immediately suspected him and his companion, another resident alien from Mexico named Salomón Graham. "They just didn't fit," Corbett said. "Their motives were wrong." Fife said he learned from refugees, who were familiar with *orejas* (Spanish for "ears," a slang word for spies) that Cruz and Graham were probably government infiltrators. The group held several meetings to decide what to do. "I felt that if he was a real volunteer—and we couldn't rule that out completely—we would be making a terrible mistake to exclude him," Corbett said. Another consideration—at least in Corbett's mind—was a government study he'd read about that said 20 percent of informants are converted by the groups they infiltrate. The task force had made a commitment long before to be as open and above-board as possible, so they decided to give Cruz and Graham the benefit of the doubt. The only allowance they made for the possibility that the two men were spies was to keep from them specific times and locations of crossings. In Nogales, however, Socorro Aguilar and Father Quiñones were much more open with Cruz, involving him in several surreptitious entries of Central Americans into the United States.

Jack Elder, the director of Casa Oscar Romero in South Texas, was arrested in April 1984 for transporting three Salvadorans to the bus station the month before. Six months later, while Elder was still awaiting trial, he and Stacey Merkt were indicted again, on different charges of aiding the illegal entry of aliens and transporting them within the country. Merkt was arrested for violating her probation, and the Catholic Diocese of Brownsville raised the $25,000 cash needed for her bail. Trials on the two incidents were set for January and February 1985. Lawyer Stephen Cooper of the Neighborhood Justice Center in St. Paul, Minnesota, took on Merkt's and Elder's case. By this time, sanctuary had enough support for a public solicitation of funds, and the National Sanctuary Defense Fund, an independent, San Francisco-based organization founded in the summer of 1984 to raise legal defense money for sanctuary workers, agreed to pay the costs of their defense.

These arrests, rather than intimidating sanctuary's supporters, encouraged many who had previously been silent to speak out. Catholic Bishop Joseph Fiorenza of Galveston-Houston joined Bishop John Fitzpatrick of the Brownsville, Texas, diocese in denouncing Merkt and Elder's arrest. The General Assembly of the reunited Presbyterian Church, the Board of National Ministries of the American Baptist Church (USA), the Mennonite Central Committee, the American Friends Service Committee, Clergy and Laity Concerned, the American Lutheran Church, the Methodist Federation of Social Action, the National Council of Churches, the Rabbinical Assembly, the United Church of Christ, the National Federation of Priests' Councils (representing 33,000 Catholic priests), and dozens of other Protestant, Catholic, Jewish, peace, social justice, and immigrant-rights organizations had endorsed sanctuary by the end of 1984.

In Tucson, the TEC task force was busy preparing for the national symposium. They knew the government was planning a crackdown, but they didn't know when or in what way. Fife had heard in November that a grand jury was convening in Texas to investigate the movement. Whatever was ahead, the TEC task force no longer feared arrest. Much had changed since Southside was a lone voice crying in the desert on the second anniversary of Archbishop

Romero's assassination. The Tucson sanctuary workers now had the strength of some two hundred religious congregations, a half-dozen college campuses, the cities of Cambridge, Massachusetts, and Berkeley, California, and an estimated six hundred other religious organizations nationwide behind them. The stage was set for a major confrontation with the government.

Speak Truth
To Power

JANUARY 14, 1985

At 8 sharp on a sunny, Monday morning, several Border Patrol cars and a locksmith's van bounced in a cloud of dust down Flanwill Street. The vehicles stopped where the road ended in a frost-covered yard, and several men leaped out, heading for the mobile home where Jim and Pat Corbett had lived the previous summer. Only after waking the young couple inside did the border patrolmen discover that their search warrant had been incorrectly addressed. Confused, they went back to their cars and stood in the chill air until Pat Corbett came out of a house on the east side of the property and asked them to leave. They did. The agents' failure to execute a search of Corbett's house portended the fate of the government's whole case against him.

Across town, the Border Patrol had also just paid John Fife a visit. He'd invited them in, offered coffee, and struck up a conversation, all in an effort to give the refugees in the church time to get away. But the agents had no warrant for Southside Presbyterian or any of the church buildings, including Fife's house. After he stalled them for about ten minutes, they left. "I'll bet they thought I was crazy," Fife laughed to Corbett when he called a few minutes later.

At the same time as Fife and Corbett were talking about their indictments, more Border Patrol agents were searching the house of another sanctuary worker in Tucson. Kay Kelly, a widow in her sixties who was a deacon at Southside Church, had for several months been sheltering Juana Beatriz Alvarez, a Guatemalan refugee whom Corbett had helped to enter the country the previous July. By chance, Alvarez wasn't home when the government came to arrest her. She had gone to her birthday party at a Salvadoran friend's house the night before and stayed over. Alvarez's narrow escape was another major blow to the case against Corbett.

Back at his house, Corbett put all his notes and papers into boxes and wondered whether to risk carrying them across the street. He assumed the Border Patrol had stationed someone out front while they went to get the warrant reissued. Pat checked around and saw no one; so Corbett took everything over to Barry Lazarus, a jeweler who was renting what had been the refugees' apartment. The Corbetts spent the rest of the morning sitting around the wood stove in their living room, talking with reporter Mark Turner and photographer Ron Medvescek of the *Arizona Daily Star*. The *Star*, Tucson's morning newpaper, had sent Medvescek and reporter Carmen Duarte with Corbett when he brought Juana Alvarez into the country, and it was possible the government might subpoena one or both of them to testify. The four talked, petted the dogs and cats and kittens (from the Humane Society, where Pat had taken a part-time job), and waited. The Border Patrol never came back.

In Phoenix, at 10 A.M., U.S. Attorney A. Melvin McDonald held a press conference to announce the indictments of sixteen people. He said they had been charged with conspiracy and seventy individual counts of recruiting, smuggling, transporting, and harboring illegal aliens. McDonald termed it a "simple alien-smuggling case." Flanked by Harold Ezell, Western Regional Commissioner for the Immigration and Naturalization Service, Ruth Anne Myers, INS District Director in Phoenix, and Donald M. Reno, Jr., the Special Assistant U.S. Attorney who would prosecute the case, McDonald said the indictments were the result of a ten-month probe, using undercover agents and informants wearing concealed tape recorders, into the activities of the sanctuary movement in Tucson, Nogales, and Phoenix.

Besides Fife and Corbett, the indictment named the following members of the TEC task force on Central America: Phil Willis-Conger, the project director, who had recently married and added Willis to his name; Katherine Flaherty, a volunteer from Washington, D.C., who had been arrested with Willis-Conger the previous March; Peggy Hutchison, a graduate student in Middle Eastern Studies at the University of Arizona who also served as director of border ministry for Tucson Metropolitan Ministries, a social service organization of the United Methodist Church; and Nena MacDonald, a Quaker nurse from Lubbock, Texas, who had worked briefly with the task force during the summer of 1984.

The indicted from Nogales were Father Ramón Quiñones and Socorro Aguilar, who, as Mexican citizens, were not under the jurisdiction of U.S. courts but agreed to be tried nevertheless; a young priest from Iowa, Father Anthony Clark, who had replaced Father Noriega at Sacred Heart Catholic Church in 1983; and Mary K. Doan Espinoza, a 32-year-old mother of four, the daughter of a former mayor of Nogales, Arizona, director of religious education for parochial schools in that town, and a volunteer at Sacred Heart.

The indictment named six people from Phoenix, three of whom were nuns. Sister Darlene Nicgorski, a member of the Milwaukee-based School Sisters of St. Francis, had been a teacher in Guatemala when the assassination of her pastor in 1981 forced her to flee. In 1984, Nicgorski went to work as border representative for the Chicago Religious Task Force on Central America, arranging transportation for refugees to churches around the country. Sister Mary Waddell and Sister Anna Priester, of the Sisters of Charity of the Blessed Virgin Mary, were also indicted, as was Wendy LeWin, a young woman who had worked for the government resettling Cuban refugees and who now volunteered at the Central American Refugee Project in Phoenix. The last two indictees from Phoenix were Salvadoran citizens: Bertha Martel-Benavides, a laundry worker, and Cecilia del Carmen Juarez de Emory, a housewife. No one in the TEC task force knew who these two women were, and they pleaded guilty to a reduced charge and were dropped from the indictment soon after it was announced. The government also dismissed charges against Sisters Waddell and Priester, bringing the number of defendants down to twelve.

McDonald announced this January morning that twenty-five more people had been named as "unindicted co-conspirators." He said these were members of the conspiracy who could have been charged but were not. Among them were Father Elford, Kay Kelly, Ellen Willis-Conger (Phil's wife), Donovan Cook, pastor of University Baptist Church in Seattle, and Tim Nonn, who had returned from seminary in San Francisco and rejoined the TEC task force in 1984. Any one of them might be called to testify in the case. Another fifty-five Guatemalan and Salvadoran nationals who'd passed through Tucson between March and November of 1984 were designated "illegal alien unindicted co-conspirators." As the government's main witnesses against the sanctuary workers, they would be granted immunity from prosecution (although not from deportation), and this morning, in addition to Tucson, the INS had arrested people in Phoenix, Seattle, Philadelphia, and Rochester. The sweeps were conducted without going into churches; most of the Central Americans were not in sanctuary, and of those who were, some were caught when they went outside. Refugees who stayed inside the church building, such as one Salvadoran couple at Riverside Church in Manhattan, were left alone.

Along with the indictment, Prosecutor Donald Reno presented a 31-page pretrial memo, in which he outlined the strategies he expected the defense to employ. He said he anticipated they would raise four main arguments: (1) the aliens were entitled to come here, (2) the sanctuary workers had no specific intent to break the law, (3) the Reagan Administration's Central America policy was immoral, and (4) the defendants' religious beliefs required them to protect those fleeing war-torn countries. Reno said he had already filed a motion asking the court to rule out those defenses.

The prosecutor had reason to expect the court to decide in his favor. In the one previous sanctuary case to date, that of Stacey Merkt, Judge Filemon Vela had ruled that neither her religion nor U.S. policy in Central America had any relevance to the charges of alien-smuggling. The government sought to try these cases on the narrowest grounds possible, and federal judges were willing to assist them in that effort. Reno quoted from a 1984 federal court decision cited in his pre-trial memo: "The asylum question is really political and essentially a matter of foreign policy, the conduct of which is committed to the executive and legislative branches of our government—not to the courts in a case such as this."

"If the defendants have a *bona fide* belief in the need for asylum, then the procedures to fill that need are no more complicated than applying for a driver's license," Reno said. When reporters asked about the near-blanket denial of Salvadoran and Guatemalan asylum petitions, he answered, "The courts must then be sending a message as to the validity of their position."

The massive scope of the indictments caught many in the TEC task force by surprise. "I thought a grand jury would have been a more convenient way for them to salt people away," Jim Corbett said, referring to a commitment made by most sanctuary workers to go to jail rather than testify against each other or against refugees. He really hadn't expected the government to go to all the trouble and expense of a "show trial."

When John Fife saw the Border Patrol at his door, he thought, "Well, we're finally going to get to it." He had long anticipated a legal test of sanctuary, and now his main concern was that it would be fair. Marianne Fife was relieved at the indictment; "I never knew under what circumstances it was going to happen," she said. "I imagined awful things—planting drugs, or making John look like he was doing something ugly. But once it happened, I relaxed completely." Her sons were older now, and, knowing what was ahead, she could accept it.

Nationwide, the arrests breathed new life into the movement. Many religious leaders expressed outrage at the government's use of concealed tape recorders in churches, and there was an outpouring of support for the indicted and their families. The Roman Catholic Bishops of Tucson, Phoenix, and Gallup, New Mexico, issued a joint statement saying sanctuary was "a moral position, publicly affirmed." The National Council of Churches condemned the arrests. Registration for the TEC task force's symposium, scheduled for the following weekend, jumped from 300 to 1,500 participants. The symposium brought clergy, academics, refugees, theologians, lawyers, and sanctuary workers to Temple Emanu-El in Tucson for five days of discussion and spiritual reflection. Timed as it was on the heels of the indictments, the symposium became a reaffirmation of the importance of sanctuary.

Author, historian, and Holocaust survivor Elie Wiesel, awarded the Nobel Peace Prize in 1986, was the honored guest at the Inter-American Symposium on Sanctuary. Wiesel avoided specific endorsement of the movement, saying he did not wish to inject himself in politics, but he did give a moving, personal account of what it is like to be a refugee. Gary MacEoin spoke on the legal aspects of the refugee crisis. Rev. William Sloane Coffin, pastor of Riverside Church in New York City, discussed the nature of the conflict in Central America and quoted John F. Kennedy: "Those who make peaceful evolution impossible make violent revolution inevitable." A Salvadoran minister and a Mayan-Quiché Indian from Guatemala gave their perspectives on Central America, and several Biblical scholars delivered papers on the theological nature of sanctuary. Jim Corbett, who some at the seminar were treating like a saint, tried to "demythologize" himself by announcing that he didn't believe in God.

"I'm an unbeliever," Corbett told the group. "That is, I don't believe selfhood survives death, and I consider any conceivable God to be an idol. As I read the Bible, this kind of unbelief is entirely consistent with the faith of Abraham and Moses and achieves classic expression in Job. The Book of Job rejects belief in reward or punishment as a support for the covenant faith. In opposition to the self-serving religion of his friends, Job insists that the person who serves to actualize *shalom* must be ready to suffer."

Shalom, which Corbett translated as "harmonious community," was another word for "living the Kingdom." In his study of the Old Testament, Corbett had found a faith that was not dependent on any belief in afterlife or a God that would set things right on Judgment Day. He continued:

Gathering to seek guidance, we find that Scripture and other prophecy address us primarily as a community and call for a community response. We are to live together in ways that hallow the earth with peace and justice, and this power is not in the state, nor is it in money, nor does it come from the barrel of a gun. Rather, we are empowered to participate whenever we form into congregations that seek to hear and do *torah*; individuals can and should resist injustice, but only in community can we do justice. In an unredeemed world, we are all refugees in need of congregational sanctuary.

Corbett's discovery that sanctuary resembled the ancient Hebrew concept of community prompted him to study the works of more modern Jewish philosophers, such as Martin Buber. He and Pat also began attending Friday night services at Temple Emanu-El. The Corbetts were still Quakers, but they now saw themselves as more Jewish than Christian and more "unbelievers" than either.

Heartened by the broad-based ecumenical support for sanctuary, members of the Tucson and Chicago task forces sat down and discussed their differences in a renewed spirit of togetherness. They agreed that sanctuary was, first and foremost, a movement for refugees, and they also agreed to maintain its diverse, grass-roots nature. Although the two sides remained poles apart, they decided to discontinue their public debate. The prospect of a major court test served to temporarily unify the movement.

At the same time that sanctuary leaders were mending fences in Tucson, Jack Elder, director of Casa Oscar Romero in San Benito, Texas, was on trial for driving three Salvadorans to the bus station the previous March. U.S. District Judge Hayden Head, Jr., allowed the jury at the Corpus Christi trial to consider religious convictions as a motive, and after two hours of deliberation, they acquitted Elder. Jurors later said they felt the government had not proven that Elder was "furthering" the aliens' illegal presence, a requirement for conviction on a transporting charge. "This is a simple little situation where a man gives a ride three miles down the road," Stephen Cooper, Elder's lawyer, said in his closing. Elder, a Vietnam veteran and former Peace Corps volunteer in Costa Rica, still faced trial with Stacey Merkt on other charges. In that trial, held in Houston in February, Judge Filemon Vela forbade Steve Cooper from using religious motivation or U.S. refugee law as defenses. The jury convicted Merkt of conspiracy and Elder of all six charges against him. In March, Judge Vela revoked Merkt's earlier probation, sentenced her to 179 days in prison, and ordered her to disassociate herself from Casa Romero and not to speak publicly about sanctuary while her case was on appeal. Vela wanted to sentence Elder to two years' probation with the same restrictions, but, when Elder said he would not be able to abide by those restrictions, the judge angrily gave him one year in jail. The next day, Vela reduced the sentence to 150 days in a halfway house in San Antonio. During the sentencing, Judge Vela said, "I speak as a person who agrees with the sanctuary movement, [but I want to] assure everybody in this country that the integrity of the legal system will be preserved. This is the lightest sentence I have ever given in a transporting case." To Merkt, Vela said, "I admire your motivation. I have nothing but respect for you." To Elder, he said, "You're a good person."

Rather than slowing or stopping the movement, Merkt's and Elder's convictions and the Arizona indictments served only to increase its visibility. The number of sanctuary churches climbed to 225, and the movement garnered endorsements from several major Catholic religious orders during the first five months of 1985. The Maryknoll Sisters, Brothers, Fathers, and lay Missionaries came forward to support the indicted, as did the chapters of the western provinces of the Franciscans and the Redemptorists. (The Catholic Bishops as a group still refrained from making an endorsement; Corbett said he believed this was because of the close Catholic connection with government-financed refugee programs.) Later in the year, the Reform Judaism assembly added its name to the list of national religious bodies endorsing the movement. It seemed that whatever government officials did, they could not stop the spread of sanctuary.

There was one thing the government could do that would, in the words of John Fife, "put sanctuary out of business tomorrow." But that one thing the government would not do: grant extended voluntary departure to Salvadoran and Guatemalan refugees. In April 1985, the U.S. Senate judiciary subcommittee held hearings on the question of EVD for Salvadorans. Elliott Abrams, then Assistant Secretary of State for Human Rights and Humanitarian Affairs, restated the government's position: Salvadorans came here for economic, not political, reasons, there was no evidence of deportees suffering persecution, and the asylum process was fair and impartial. INS Commissioner Alan Nelson gave these arguments and added another: Granting EVD to Salvadorans could "lead to an invasion of feet people magnifying the migration from that region, making what we already see as a stream become a torrent."

According to Gary MacEoin in *No Promised Land*, the U.S. government had long raised the specter of brown hordes as a reason not to comply with international standards on treatment of refugees. MacEoin cited the 1980 Reagan Task Force on Immigration warning of the "demographic consequences" of increasing the percentage of "Hispanics" in the United States. In 1985, the administration agreed to admit 70,000 more refugees than the normal ceiling of 270,000, but only 3,000 of these could be from Latin America (the vast majority, 59,000, were to be from the Soviet Union, Eastern Europe, and Indochina). "These are the official ceilings; actual admissions are even more imbalanced," wrote Arthur Helton of the Lawyers' Committee for International Human Rights in a *New York Times* editorial on April 2, 1985. "In 1984, for example, only 93 Salvadorans and no Guatemalans were admitted as refugees." An additional 328 Salvadorans (2.45 percent of the adjudicated cases) and three Guatemalans (0.39 percent) were granted political asylum in 1984. And that was a year in which more than one million Salvadorans and Guatemalans were living in refugee camps or in hiding outside their countries.

As Corbett pointed out, the threat of an "invasion of feet people" was a red-herring. The sanctuary workers were talking about certifiable political refugees, which the U.S. government was legally bound to protect. Elliott Abrams himself said, "Legally and morally, the distinction between economic migrants and political refugees matters greatly." Compared to the millions of undocumented workers who came to the United States every year seeking a better way of life, the number of political refugees from El Salvador and Guatemala was small.

Another administration objection to Latin American immigrants was apparently based on the contention that the United States did not need any more poor or unskilled people. Immigrants with marketable skills, especially those from communist countries, had a much better chance of getting legal status. Corbett said this was a case of our foreign policy coming home to haunt us; if the United States were more interested in economic development and redistribution of land, and less interested in militarization as a solution to El Salvador's and Guatemala's problems, the citizens of those countries would stay home. After meeting hundreds of Salvadoran and Guatemalan refugees, Corbett was convinced that the vast majority of them preferred their own country, language, and culture, and would go back, if conditions were such that they did not risk death, torture, or imprisonment by doing so.

The anti-Latin bias of U.S. government policy aside, the primary reason for wholesale denial of temporary safe haven to Salvadorans and Guatemalans remained political: we could not call governments we supported gross violators of human rights. In 1984, Jim Corbett also became aware of another reason: the Pentagon's Central America strategy depended on there being no place for these people to run to. "During recent months," Corbett said at the sanctuary symposium, "refugees have surged out of El Salvador. They report massacres by the military that are beyond anything previously suffered. Most of these mass murders are perpetrated by aerial attack in areas that are now free-fire zones. The idea is to use military assault to uproot the people and then to force the survivors into 'model villages' under strict military supervision. The process is called 'pacification.' The violation of refugee rights is integral to the use of this strategy, because military pacification won't work if the refugees it creates have an alternative to model villages."

There can be no doubt that the denial of extended voluntary departure to Salvadorans was very important to the Reagan administration. In the fall of 1986, a Republican Senator said in closed session that the President would not sign the Simpson-Rodino immigration reform act, which he supported, as long as it contained a

provision granting EVD to Salvadorans and Nicaraguans. The provision was removed, and the President signed the legislation. The
DeConcini-Moakley bill, which also would have provided EVD to
Salvadorans, died in committee without ever coming to a vote. Massachusetts Congressman Joe Moakley vowed to reintroduce it in the
next session of Congress, but John Fife, who had kept a close eye
on the progress of DeConcini-Moakley, said, even if it passed, there
would not be enough votes to override a presidential veto.

Despite this discouraging picture, Jim Corbett continued his efforts to make the system work. In May 1985, while in Phoenix for
the first of several pretrial hearings, Corbett and Pat had lunch with
Ruth Anne Myers, INS District Director, and Mark Turner, of the
Arizona Daily Star. Turner wrote an article about the lunch, titled
"Defendant, INS officer break bread together," in which Myers was
quoted as saying that the policy in her district is not to arrest undocumented immigrants who voluntarily come in to an INS office
to apply for asylum. Corbett said he considered this assurance a
breakthrough, since he had not received it when he had a lawyer call
the Tucson INS office for two Nicaraguans in December. He said
he would begin advising refugees that "affirmative filing" was once
again a possibility.

The legality of affirmative filing received another boost in June,
when a Fifth Circuit Court of Appeals overturned Stacey Merkt's
first conviction. The three-judge panel ruled that, if Merkt was on
her way to present the Salvadorans to apply for asylum, she did not
have the requisite criminal intent. (Merkt was taking the Salvadorans to San Antonio, where INS officials permitted affirmative filing,
which was not possible to the south. The appeals court disagreed
with Judge Vela's ruling that she must take people to the nearest INS
office in order not to be furthering their illegal presence.) Corbett
took Ruth Anne Myers's assurance and the Fifth Circuit's ruling to
mean that affirmative filing was now recognized as legal and that
sanctuary workers caught taking undocumented people in to apply for asylum would not be prosecuted. Later in the summer, he
began calling ahead to the Tucson office to tell them that people
were coming in from the border to apply for asylum. He hoped this
demonstration of good faith would prevent the arrests of sanctuary
workers and refugees caught en route to an INS office. In keeping

with the Quaker testimony of truth-telling, Corbett also insisted that no one say they were taking refugees in to apply for asylum unless they actually were.

U.S. District Judge Earl H. Carroll, the judge chosen at random to hear the case of the twelve sanctuary workers, issued a series of pre-trial rulings throughout the summer and fall. In June, Carroll ruled out religious motivation as a defense, saying, "Religious leaders have the same obligation as all citizens to comply with the law." Defendants and their lawyers had expected this, but they remained hopeful that the judge would allow at least one of the other defenses the government wanted excluded. Carroll also ruled that the government had the right to use undercover informants and concealed tape recorders in churches. Later in the summer, Judge Carroll moved the trial to Tucson, as the defense had requested, and suppressed any evidence gathered in Phil Willis-Conger's 1984 arrest. The judge's most crucial evidentiary rulings, however, did not come down until after jury selection had begun.

A month before the trial, Alejandro Hernández, whom Corbett had met briefly at El Centro on May 27, 1981, was granted political asylum. Hernández, who now worked as a custodian at St. Mark's Presbyterian, had fled El Salvador with his wife and young baby after his father, brother, and uncle were killed. He was the first of the more than 1,500 Salvadorans whom the TEC task force had helped to apply for asylum since 1981 to receive it. One Guatemalan of hundreds aided by the TEC had received asylum in these five years. The INS was appealing the decision.

OCTOBER 24, 1985

Reporters began lining up in front of the courthouse at 5:30 A.M. At this hour, downtown Tucson's streets were empty and cold. The city was in a period of transition in the fall of 1985. A few blocks away, a twenty-three–story skyscraper was under construction, and federal, state, and local governments had built several modern office buildings. But in the area around the four-story federal courthouse, many of the storefronts were boarded up, and others sold discount goods. Tucson still lacked the sophistication of a big city.

By 8:00, when the marshalls opened the brass front doors, the line snaked around the corner onto Broadway. Print boys—self-serious reporters from AP, UPI, the *Arizona Daily Star*, the *Tucson Citizen*, and the *Arizona Republic*—held the front. Television news people, reporters for the national papers, volunteers at the Arizona Sanctuary Defense Fund media office, and local well-wishers, many of whom were clergy or retired, followed. During these first few days of the trial, there was great competition for the eighty-four seats in the courtroom.

The defendants were surrounded by reporters and cameras as they walked to court. Jim and Pat Corbett, in cords and cloth coats, were accompanied by Corbett's mother, a spry, tiny, 84-year-old. Gladys Corbett had spent the years since her husband's death driving her motor home to horse shows around the country. She attended the trial faithfully, often getting in line with reporters early in the morning. Pat Corbett quit her job so she could come to court every day. She passed the time drawing animal caricatures of the judge, lawyers, prosecutor, and witnesses. Marianne Fife missed most of the trial because she had to work. As she walked with John this morning, she looked businesslike, her blond hair bobbed. John Fife, like Corbett, had aged noticeably in the past few years; his hair and beard, shorter than in 1981, were now tinged with gray.

No cameras or tape recorders were allowed in the courtroom, and as Fife passed through the metal detector in the lobby, he took off his watch and held his belt buckle sideways to avoid setting off the machine. In the anteroom, he paused to smoke one last cigarette and kid with reporters. His sense of humor and easygoing manner made him popular with the local journalists, many of whom were put off by the quiet seriousness of the other defendants.

The local reporters saw the trial as more of a job than many of the network and national correspondents, who were following the story out of personal interest. Sanctuary had a dramatic, human interest appeal for writers that went beyond its value as a news story. Some reporters, such as Dale Maharidge of the *Sacramento Bee*, had traveled through Mexico with Corbett and developed a friendship with him. Just by covering the story, journalists risked criminal prosecution—so they were, in a sense, "co-conspirators." These writers were more knowledgeable about sanctuary than those who'd just been assigned to the trial, but they also may have had more trouble maintaining their objectivity. Chris Medvescek, a Quaker free-lance journalist and the wife of photographer Ron Medvescek,

had written about sanctuary for the *Christian Science Monitor* and
other national publications in the past, but she declined to cover the
trial out of concern that she could not do it objectively. The problem was not confined to national correspondents; halfway through
the trial, *Arizona Daily Star* reporter Mark Turner asked to be re-
assigned for similar reasons. The compelling nature of the refugees'
stories, the movement's long-standing cultivation of the media, as
well as Donald Reno's reticence to comment on the proceedings,
all contributed to coverage that was generally more favorable to the
defense than to the prosecution.

The twelve defendants were now eleven. A few days before the
trial began, Katherine Flaherty, citing family pressures, had pleaded
guilty to a misdemeanor in exchange for dismissal of the felony
counts against her. Flaherty was given probation and went home
to Washington, D.C. According to John Fife and Sister Darlene
Nicgorski, the prosecutor had offered every defendant a similar plea-
bargain arrangement early in October. All the government wanted,
the defendants realized, was for them to admit they'd broken the
law. But to do so, as Corbett said, "would concede the destruction
of refugee laws." The defendants agreed they would not say they'd
broken the law, and they would not say the refugees were illegal
aliens—even if they had to go to jail for it.

The defendants enjoyed some of the best legal talent in the country. Fife was represented by Robert Hirsh, a prominent criminal
defense lawyer from Tucson. James Brosnahan, of the San Francisco
firm of Morrison and Foerster, represented Socorro Aguilar. Ellen
Yaroshefsky, from the Center for Constitutional Rights in New York
City, represented Wendy LeWin. A. Bates Butler, III, the former U.S.
Attorney for Arizona who had represented Phil Willis-Conger after
his first arrest in 1984, was representing him again in this case. Jim
Corbett's lawyer, Steve Cooper, was the only other attorney who'd
defended sanctuary workers before. (Corbett also had Barbara Elfbrandt as his local counsel, but she participated in the trial only one
day.)

The defense attorneys operated without a clear-cut leader. Hirsh
and Brosnahan conducted most of the questioning, and the other
lawyers took turns asking questions of particular relevance to their
clients. At the time the lawyers wanted to work as a team, but, after

the trial, Hirsh said he believed the lack of leadership had worked against them. "There were too many of us," he said. "No one lawyer was able to develop any personality dominance, or influence over the jury. It also looked like we were ganging up on Reno." The prosecutor and his co-counsel, 27-year-old Assistant U.S. Attorney Joan Grabowski, sat in front of the jury box, across from the battery of defense lawyers and their clients.

"All rise!" The bailiff summoned the courtroom to order, and the judge, a white-haired man of 61, entered in a swirl of black robes. "United States District Court for the district of Arizona is now in session, the Honorable Earl H. Carroll presiding!" Today was jury selection, and as the first group of prospective jurors filed in, the defendants, their lawyers, and prosecutors stood. They performed this ritual throughout the trial, whenever the jury went in or out. The judge remained seated.

The clerk swore the jury candidates in, and Judge Carroll introduced himself, the prosecutors, the defense lawyers, and the defendants. He pointed out that two of the defendants were priests, one was a minister, and one was a nun. (Sister Nicgorski was the only one of the four not dressed in religious garb throughout the trial. Her lawyer later reminded the jury that modern nuns don't necessarily wear habits.) Carroll explained that the jury's function was to decide what the facts were, and it was his job to tell them what law applied to those facts. The jurors were then sent out and brought back individually for questioning.

One of those called this morning was Catherine Sheaffer, a prim, dark-haired woman with librarian glasses who described herself as being from a "government family." She was a college graduate with a year of law school who'd been laid off from her job administering federal grants four months before. She'd been "on vacation" from newspapers and television since. "I have tried not to get involved in anything," she said.

Judge Carroll asked what she had heard about sanctuary.

"I think they were Salvadorans—I guess being persecuted—smuggled into the United States," Sheaffer said.

"Could good motives justify violating the law?"

"I would take the responsibility that goes with breaking the law. That's how I try to raise my children."

"Do you go to church?"

"Yes, Christ Community Church. I don't believe our church gets involved in social issues. It's a Scriptural-teaching church."

"Would you have any trouble returning a verdict of guilty against religious clergy and lay workers?"

"No."

At the morning recess, the defendants and their lawyers went into a room to discuss the candidates. Catherine Sheaffer elicited the most debate. Many of the defendants were concerned about her religious fundamentalism, and their lawyers worried about her year in law school. But a friend of one of the lawyer's wives worked in the county clerk's office, and she came up with the information that Sheaffer had recently changed her party affiliation from Republican to Democrat. That, coupled with Sheaffer's having been laid off, led defense lawyers to think she was dissatisfied with the government. They decided to allow her on the panel.

The final jury was all white, overwhelmingly female (only three of the twelve were men), and almost completely ignorant of the sanctuary movement. None spoke Spanish. Besides Sheaffer, they included a widowed Catholic nurse, a computer programmer at Hughes Aircraft, a musician, a cafeteria worker at Hughes, a crossing guard, and a military wife. One of the men, a city building inspector who had spent four years in the Navy building missile tracking systems, said the first time he'd heard about sanctuary was "when people were perishing in the desert." He talked about the Salvadorans who died in Organ Pipe monument in 1980. "I told my family—it's terrible that people have to die like that. They should be able to get in in orderly fashion." The judge asked if the memory of the desert incident would influence him. He said it wouldn't. Another juror, a young man with a tattoo on his arm, told Judge Carroll that he'd heard about a benefit rock concert for the Arizona Sanctuary Defense Fund, "but I thought sanctuary was something for birds."

Amid laughter, the judge responded, "There is a comment there, but I won't pick that up, either."

Defense lawyers had complained before that Carroll was biased against them; this remark only fueled their suspicions. During pre-trial hearings, Carroll had made several comments that indicated to the defense that he'd already found their clients guilty. At one point, Carroll asked when else in American history a religious leader had stood on the steps of the courthouse, then walked over to his church and announced he was going to violate the law. When Ellen Yaroshefsky suggested that Martin Luther King, Jr., had done that, Carroll answered that King had spent his time in jail and, in any event, these defendants were not of the same character as King. Defense lawyers also objected to the way Carroll had described the case to the jury: "the so-called sanctuary movement," "in simplest terms, an alien smuggling case," and the like. After his "sanctuary is for the birds" rejoinder, the defense asked Carroll, for the first of many times, to remove himself as trial judge. He refused.

Judge Carroll decided not to impose a gag order, although he did forbid demonstrations, sound trucks, or television cameras within 100 feet of the courthouse. He also chose not to sequester the jury, giving instead the same admonition at the end of every day: "Do not look at, listen to, or read anything connected with this case, and do not discuss anything that happens here among yourselves or with anyone else." Judge Carroll was kindly, even fatherly, to them. Catherine Sheaffer smiled at him. (Defense lawyers assumed that some jurors would ignore the instruction not to read or talk about the case. Most said later they had scrupulously followed it.)

The day after the jury was impaneled, Judge Carroll was about to leave the bench when a man in the gallery stood, turned, and slapped two bloody handprints high on the courtroom wall. "The blood of Central America is on our hands, because we are our brothers' and sisters' keepers!" he shouted.

"Let's escort the gentleman out," the judge said and disappeared into chambers. The marshalls hustled the offender away and cleared the courtroom. Outside, the man handed out a press release and told reporters that the blood on the wall was his own, drawn earlier and secreted into the courtroom in a plastic vial. He also said he'd waited until the jury was in the other room, so that he wouldn't cause a mistrial. It was the one public outburst of the whole proceeding.

NOVEMBER 12, 1985

Several days into jury selection, Judge Carroll came out with a series of rulings that essentially eliminated any defense of sanctuary. On October 25, and then again on October 28, Carroll issued new orders and reiterated earlier ones that said he would allow no evidence on conditions in Central America, international law, U.S. asylum policies, good or bad motive, "good faith," "mistake of law" (the defendants' contention that what they were doing was legal), or "necessity" (the argument that the defendants had to break a lesser law in order to prevent a greater crime). For various reasons, Judge Carroll found all of these arguments irrelevant to the charge of alien smuggling. The necessity defense wasn't valid, he said, because the aliens suffered no imminent threats to their lives or freedom in Mexico, and they didn't turn themselves in to the INS at the border like they were supposed to. International law was out because the Geneva Conventions and Nuremberg Principles weren't "self-executing," and, in any case, they didn't apply to people who entered the United States surreptitiously. Judge Carroll had accepted the government's contention that only the Attorney General had the right to decide who is a refugee and who is an illegal alien.

These sweeping orders were a bitter disappointment to the defendants. "He didn't even want to listen," Corbett said, to what the defendants believed was irrefutable proof that refugees *did* suffer imminent threats to their lives or freedom in Mexico and that Guatemalans and Salvadorans who attempted to apply for asylum at the U.S. border were arrested and turned over to Mexican officials for deportation. The defendants also contended that the Geneva Convention that forbids deporting civilians back to a war zone was ratified by the U.S. Congress and so, under Article VI of the Constitution, had the force of law in this country. Lastly, the sanctuary workers said, it's just not true that any undocumented person not presented to the INS is an illegal alien. Many of those aided had letters from the U.N. High Commissioner for Refugees designating them as refugees, and the UNHCR Handbook plainly stated: "Recognition of his refugee status does not make [a person] a refugee but declares him to be one. He does not become a refugee because of recognition, but is recognized because he is a refugee."

Judge Carroll argued that while some of the aliens involved in the case may have been refugees, they were not guaranteed resettlement in the United States. The only real defense he left open was if the sanctuary workers could say they didn't know that a person hadn't been presented to the INS. If that were the case, they did not "knowingly and willfully" break the law. But the point was they *did* know —they knew they couldn't present a person to the INS because to do so would only speed up his or her deportation. And that point they were not allowed to explain.

The judge had the sanctuary workers in the same Catch-22 that the INS had had Salvadorans and Guatemalans in since 1980. Carroll's rulings ensured that real questions raised by sanctuary —whether the U.S. government was violating refugee rights, or whether Corbett and the others had any recourse to going around the law—would not even be considered by the jury. This, more than having no defense, was the defendants' greatest frustration. They realized it would be several more years, at least, before an American jury would be allowed to hear a complete and truthful presentation of the situation that gave rise to the sanctuary movement.

"It looks like Judge Carroll is running his own railroad," Fife told reporters.

Federal judges are forbidden from talking about their cases or rulings, but Tucson attorney Thomas Chandler, who called himself a good friend of Carroll's, offered some insight into the judge's thinking. "You don't try causes in court," Chandler said. "You try the guilt or innocence of particular defendants." Like Judge Vela in Texas, Carroll apparently did not wish to get into questions that were the exclusive province of the executive branch: foreign policy, refugee admissions, and asylum procedures.

The defense debated how to proceed. "We were done for," Hirsh said. "All we could do was rely on jury nullification." Jury nullification referred to the power of juries to reject the law and decide the case on their conscience. The problem with it, as a legal strategy, was that in federal courts and all but two state courts lawyers weren't allowed to tell juries that they had this right. Even assuming that the jury didn't want to convict the sanctuary workers, the defense had to give them some legal basis on which to acquit.

"When you have no way to go," Hirsh said, "and you've got a case where the defendants haven't done anything so wicked as to get the jury mad at them, you have to make the government look as bad as possible." It was a negative approach, and one that conceded control of the proceedings to the government, but it was also the only one left after Carroll issued his rulings. Defense lawyers were angry at the judge for putting them in a box, and for the rest of the trial they butted heads with him at every turn.

Their initial reaction was to bombard the judge with motions, no less than six during the first week of November. All asked for a delay, a dismissal, a change of judge, or a mistrial. Some of these motions attacked Carroll's bias and the lateness of his rulings, with the defense arguing that their strategy had been "sandbagged." Other motions pointed out that former Filipino President Ferdinand Marcos's and Salvadoran President Duarte's families had been given sanctuary, so why not ordinary citizens? (Judge Carroll said those people were admitted at the discretion of the Attorney General, and therefore legally.) Another motion asked the judge to step down because he and his wife owned stock in Phelps-Dodge, an international smelting and mining company with a Salvadoran subsidiary, Conelca, connected to the case. (One of the "illegal alien unindicted co-conspirators" had been kidnapped and tortured for union organizing at Conelca. Sanctuary workers were charged with bringing his two young children into the country.) Phelps-Dodge was also one of Carroll's major clients at the Phoenix law firm of Evans, Hull, Kitchel and Jenckes, where he worked for twenty-eight years until Senator Dennis DeConcini asked President Jimmy Carter to appoint him to the federal bench in 1980. "A stockholder with a direct economic interest in the stability of El Salvador should not judge the exclusion of testimony about killings, torture, and disappearances in that country," the defense brief said. Carroll disagreed.

Of the motions filed by the defense during the first week of November, the only one that seemed to interest the judge at all was the one claiming selective prosecution. This motion argued that the sanctuary movement had been prosecuted not because it broke the law, as the government claimed, but because it was publicly outspoken in its criticism of the government's treatment of Central American refugees. Several comments by government officials had led the defense to think that this was the case. Thomas Martin, the border patrolman who attended the declaration of sanctuary at Southside Church, concluded his "Frito Bandito" memo by saying, "I believe that all political considerations should be considered before any further action is taken towards this group." Yuma Intelligence Agent Dean B. Thatcher agreed, writing on January 4, 1983: "The sanctuary movement does not appear to be a serious threat to enforcement efforts by the Service in its overall context. However, if the movement's growth is misinterpreted through lack of intelligence, the Service image could be adversely affected."

Judge Carroll decided to hear this motion argued. On the morning of November 12, he called the jury in to dismiss them for several days. The jury had been ensconced in a side room and was oblivious to Carroll's rulings and the commotion they had caused.

The defense called as their witness James Rayburn, the INS agent who had conducted the sanctuary investigation—code named Operation Sojourner. Rayburn, a Vietnam vet in his early forties, said he started keeping a file on the movement shortly after Southside declared sanctuary. In it went the *People* article on Corbett, the 60 Minutes transcript, Chicago Religious Task Force publications, and various newspaper stories. In an August 1982 memo to other INS agents, Rayburn noted the sympathetic tone of *People*'s characterization of Corbett: "The article leads out deliberately structured to draw the reader's attention to Subject Corbett's poor health and ever-present pain, purposefully to create an aura of martyrdom. This journalistic attitude continues throughout the article."

Rayburn's memos revealed that he was also keeping an eye on the movement's private activities. In mid-1983, the agent went down to Hermosillo to investigate complaints that sanctuary was cutting into the business of Mexican coyotes. Rayburn went to the Hotel Sonora —according to Corbett, the most notorious hotel in Hermosillo for forcing Central American women into prostitution—and spoke with some of the coyotes who operated out of there. They said that once in a while someone from the Red Cross in Hermosillo would show up at the hotel and take specific Salvadorans from a group they were planning to smuggle into the United States. Rayburn learned that the TEC was handling a "very low number" of aliens, perhaps ten a month.

"Due to a heavy work load and priorities set within the anti-smuggling program," Rayburn concluded his June 1983 memo, "I strongly recommended that for the present the 'El Salvadorian Underground Railroad' be assigned to a centralized intelligence office." The agent seemed to think that prosecuting the movement would only create more martyrs, and he opposed launching an investigation. For a while, his higher-ups agreed with him; INS officials in Tucson, Phoenix, and Washington all claimed during 1982 and '83 that the movement had no significant effect on their ability to enforce the law.

Then, in late 1983 or early 1984, Rayburn's bosses in the INS or the Justice Department (the INS's parent agency) changed their minds. Rayburn said he received the order to proceed with an investigation from Mark Reed, assistant to Harold Ezell, INS Western Regional Commissioner. This differed from normal practice: in every other case Rayburn had worked on, he had put in a request to investigate first. The agent went ahead and did his job, but he did not appreciate all the phone calls he was getting from Washington about the case. He wrote a letter asking his superior to tell callers to go through normal channels.

Rayburn claimed sanctuary was investigated because it fell under "Category One" of the anti-smuggling unit—a highly organized, interstate smuggling ring that brought in large quantities of aliens. He added that the INS also "prioritizes" smuggling rings that moved OTMs (Other Than Mexicans).

But, Brosnahan asked, what about the fact that Rayburn's own intelligence told him sanctuary was moving less than ten aliens a month?

"The deterrence factor was primary," Rayburn said, "not getting the most number of aliens."

"Was public awareness a factor?"

"I don't know the answer to that."

In December 1984, Rayburn continued, he and Donald Reno went to Washington to present the evidence they had gathered to, among others, INS Commissioner Alan Nelson, and INS legal counsel Maurice Inman. This trip, the abrupt turnaround in the government's position on sanctuary, the order to investigate from above, and the phone calls from Washington all indicated that the INS did not consider this just a routine alien-smuggling case. After the trial, more evidence of the government's extraordinary concern about sanctuary surfaced. In the wake of the Iran-*contra* scandal in mid-November 1986, reporters learned that the Central Intelligence Agency, Federal Bureau of Investigation, and National Security Council had been investigating sanctuary and Central American peace groups for at least three years. In a lawsuit against the FBI filed in February 1987, a former informant named Frank Varelli charged that he had been told that the Committee in Solidarity with the People of El Salvador was a terrorist organization, and he was supposed to find out what other violent groups were connected with it. But when he attended meetings in Dallas, Varelli, a naturalized citizen and Baptist minister from a conservative Salvadoran family, said he learned that CISPES members were good people, concerned about the suffering of his people and wanting a negotiated settlement to the war. This realization, he said, added to his belief that his superior had been stealing money meant for him, led to his defection from the FBI. Varelli also claimed that the FBI was responsible for breaking into Bethany House, a private residence for nuns in Dallas next to a sanctuary church. At least three dozen break-ins at sanctuary offices around the country (including Peggy Hutchison's office in Tucson) occurred during 1984 and '85. Movement members believed that the U.S. government, or agents of the Salvadoran or Guatemalan governments, committed these burglaries. In most cases, files were rifled and documents taken, including the addresses of refugees' families in El Salvador and Guatemala, but things of value were left untouched. Sanctuary workers said the burglaries were intended to frighten and intimidate them. At the Pico Rivera Methodist Church near Los Angeles, intruders cut a hole in the wall rather than go through a window or door, and at the Central American Refugee Project in Phoenix, bloody handprints were smeared on the wall. In March 1987, Assistant FBI Director Floyd Clarke told the *Chicago Tribune* that "I can tell you with certainty that there were no break-ins that were authorized, suggested, approved or considered by FBI management or supervisors." Clarke added that the Varelli case had led to changes in how FBI informants were paid.

After Rayburn stepped down, Reno presented his side. The prosecutor maintained that the investigation had been conducted for law-enforcement purposes. "The illogic of the defendants' selective prosecution argument is that by vociferously espousing their cause to the national media, they immunized themselves to criminal prosecution," he wrote in a responding brief.

Judge Carroll decided to postpone ruling on the selective prosecution motion until later. He turned down all the other defense motions and told Reno to begin presenting his case.

NOVEMBER 15, 1985

The prosecutor's strategy was evident from the first words of his opening statement. Reno wanted to dispel any sympathy the jurors might have for the Guatemalans and Salvadorans and to present the sanctuary workers as common smugglers. He always referred to the Central Americans as "aliens." Socorro Aguilar's house was "a safe house—or drop-house, in alien-smuggling parlance." The TEC task force was "a three-tiered smuggling conspiracy"—the "CEOs," or "generals," the "transporters," and the "Nogales connection." As he went through the counts he intended to prove, Reno emphasized any exchanges of money between the defendants: "Father Quiñones took the check and put it in his pocket."

Defense lawyers objected to this characterization, and, out of the presence of the jury, they argued that Reno was raising the issue of motive, which they had not been allowed to raise. "He clumsily wandered through doors that your honor had closed," Steve Cooper said. Judge Carroll disagreed, forbidding the defense from arguing an alternative motive for their clients' actions. With the defense's opening statements, however, it became clear that they intended to say as much as they could get away with.

In her opening, Ellen Yaroshefsky quoted the Reverend William Sloane Coffin: "The leader of the sanctuary movement is just beyond the reach of the immigration service." Bates Butler made reference to the "harsh" conditions at El Centro and told jurors that the INS was rejecting the refugees' asylum applications. Sister Nicgorski's attorney mentioned the assassination of her pastor and another instance in which a Guatemalan boy had his ears cut off by soldiers, which made Reno stand to object, but Judge Carroll didn't cut the lawyer off until he referred to Rayburn as an "ideologue." Three times during the defense opening statements Judge Carroll sent the jury into the other room so he could admonish the lawyers.

"That is completely outside of any order, any idea of relevance," Carroll told Ellen Yaroshefsky, in reference to her mention of the Civil War–era underground railroad. The judge warned defense lawyers that he would cite them for contempt if they continued to violate his orders. When the jury came back in, he reminded the jurors that the lawyers' statements were not to be considered as evidence.

Despite the judge's limiting instructions, defense lawyers were able to convey a great deal to the jury. Their intention was to raise the jurors' sympathy and make them realize they were only getting half the story. But Carroll stopped them so frequently that some

jurors apparently thought, as Hirsh said later, that the defense lawyers were being "sneaky dogs," trying to get around the rules of the
court. "We were too obstreperous, raised too much hell," Hirsh said.
One juror said after the trial she thought the defense's behavior was
"childish." Another said she thought the judge had been "patient"
with the defense.

NOVEMBER 21, 1985

Jesús Cruz came into court carrying the burden of the government's case. Salomón Graham, the other informant who had worked
with Cruz infiltrating the TEC, was not going to take the stand for
the prosecution. Over the summer, defense lawyers had discovered
that Graham was procuring prostitutes for migrant workers at a
farm outside Phoenix, and Reno decided not to use him as a witness.
A week before the trial began, Reno also announced he was not
going to use the tapes. The defense was surprised at this move, since
the tapes were the hard evidence the government had spent so much
time and money getting, and Reno had fought to have them admitted
during pre-trial hearings. Reno declined to say why he would not
use them, but the defense believed it was because many of the conversations about moving people from here to there were interspersed
with discussions of refugees' backgrounds, the defendants' motives,
and other inadmissable subjects. It would have been impossible for
Reno to use the tapes without some of this exculpatory evidence
coming in as well. Defense lawyers later tried to introduce all the
tapes into evidence, but Judge Carroll would not let them.

Cruz was a stout, balding man with protruding ears. As the jurors
filed in, he looked at them, the judge, or the prosecutor, but he
avoided making eye contact with the row of defendants facing him
across the room. He wore a polyester shirt over a turtleneck sweater.
In front of the bar next to the jury box, his back to reporters in the
front row, James Rayburn sat and watched Cruz for the duration of
his testimony.

The informant spoke in colloquial Spanish, and the translation
of each question and answer took a long time. Cruz was from San
Luis Potosí, Mexico, one of six children of a grocer. He had a sixth-
grade education, and, for most of his life, he had lived in Phoenix,

working variously as a farmworker, roofer, and maintenance man. He had received his resident alien card, his green card, twenty-five years earlier.

In 1978 Cruz decided to improve his fortunes by becoming a coyote. He went to work for a man named Federico Villalon, driving loads of illegal aliens from Phoenix to Florida. The first time he did it, Cruz was caught but not charged, and he went on to make another twenty to twenty-four trips to Saldivar Farms in Bonita Springs, Florida, over the next fifteen months. He took ten to twenty-seven people each time, using a motor home for larger runs. Saldivar, a tomato farmer, contracted the workers out to neighboring farms. Cruz said Villalon paid him a total of around $6,000 for his work.

In 1980, Villalon and Saldivar were arrested for running a slave camp, and Cruz was given a choice: either turn state's evidence or stand trial with his bosses. It took him only a minute to decide what to do.

Cruz went to work for Jim Rayburn at the Phoenix INS office. He became a reliable informant, completing seven or eight cases before being assigned to infiltrate the sanctuary movement. Rayburn directed him to begin his investigation with Father Quiñones, and Cruz went down to Nogales on March 27, 1984. Father Quiñones invited Cruz to go with him and Socorro Aguilar to the Sonoran prison. Cruz said Father Quiñones told the prisoners how to get to the U.S. border without being stopped by Mexican immigration. He also said the sanctuary workers coached people on how to pretend to be Mexican, so that, if they were caught, they could be sent back to Mexico and not to El Salvador or Guatemala. "He [Father Quiñones] passed around a piece of paper with names on it of persons in the U.S. who were trying to help Central Americans. He did not say they should present themselves to the U.S. immigration service."

Cruz spent almost a month on the stand. The first week, he provided a detailed account of the activities of the TEC task force in the spring, summer, and fall of 1984. He described several instances in which Father Quiñones and Phil Willis-Conger took people to a hilltop in Nogales, Sonora, and pointed out Sacred Heart Catholic Church on the other side of the border. The refugees were usually responsible for finding a hole in the fence and getting over to Sacred Heart themselves; then Cruz would drive them to Tucson or

Phoenix. Cruz also described meetings "under the cross" at South-side Church, and visits to Sister Nicgorski's apartment in Phoenix, where she was arranging transportation for people throughout the United States. The informant had little to say about Jim Corbett. Other than meetings at Southside, Cruz had seen him only two times: at Phil and Ellen Willis-Conger's wedding, and one day at Corbett's trailer, when Cruz came by to give him $46 to give to Juana Alvarez. Without telling Cruz where Alvarez was, Corbett took the government's money and told Cruz he'd give it to her.

Cruz spoke by rote, reciting names, dates, physical descriptions, locations, and conversations, as if these events had occurred the day before. He had apparently spent a great deal of time memorizing the tapes. When they began cross-examination, the defense focused on this question.

For three weeks, Hirsh, Brosnahan, and the other defense attorneys conducted what Reno later called a "withering" cross-examination. Hirsh grilled Cruz about the number of days he had spent preparing to testify. He asked the informant about how much money he had received from the government (some $18,000 since the beginning of the investigation). He got Cruz to admit he had committed perjury to protect the government in the Villalon-Saldivar trial. He brought up discrepancies between Cruz's direct testimony and transcripts of the tapes. Brosnahan emphasized the lies Cruz had told to ingratiate himself to the sanctuary workers. He pointed out that Cruz had called refugee families and told the children he wanted to send them Christmas presents, in order to get their addresses so that the INS could come arrest them. The defense tried to make Cruz look as corrupt, greedy, and amoral as possible. They did a good job of it; some jurors commented after the trial that they didn't believe a word Cruz had said. But the strategy of attacking Cruz mercilessly may also have backfired, eliciting pity for him in some jurors. "I thought of myself trying to remember a conversation that happened a year ago," said one. "I just thought he was someone doing his job," said another.

DECEMBER 10, 1985

One of the more ironic aspects of this case was the government's almost total lack of evidence against Jim Corbett. He was the man who started the whole thing, the one who had appeared in news-papers and on television all over the country proclaiming his "ille-gal" activities. Along with Fife, Corbett was presumably the defend-ant the government most wanted convicted. Yet Cruz had been unable to place Corbett at the border, or arranging transportation or shelter for anyone. Corbett's cautiousness with Cruz, and his having considerably cut down his border runs by 1984, were partly the reason why the evidence on him was so slim. More important than either of these factors, however, was the government's failure to apprehend the only real witness against him.

Reno at first hoped that Juana Alvarez's escape wouldn't damage his case too much. He wanted her declared unavailable, so that Cruz would be allowed to testify about what she had said. Normally, hearsay statements aren't allowed in court unless the person who made them is shown to be unable to testify. Reno would have to show he'd made every effort to find Alvarez to have her declared unavailable. Jim Corbett believed Reno didn't want to find her at all. It would be better for the government to have Cruz testify about her, because, if Alvarez took the stand, certain details of her past were bound to come out.

When Corbett went to counsel Alvarez in Mexico City, she told him what had happened to her. Alvarez was 32 years old and the mother of three children. Until early 1982, when her husband was kidnapped, she had lived the life of a housewife in Guatemala City.

"My husband worked 14 years in a factory," she told Corbett. "He was a member of a union local and attended meetings every Thursday. He took books and notebooks that he always guarded carefully. He never talked to me about what he was doing, so if he was doing union work or something, I don't know what it was. I think he was fired, and from pride he told me he had resigned. Then he put up a sign on the door, saying he would repair electrical appliances, because he was also an electrician. The day before he was disappeared, he took his notebooks and folder with him and came back without them. I keep dreaming that he is trying to tell me something, but I don't know what.

"Shortly after he disappeared, four men came to the house look-ing for me. They drove a luxury car that was gray with a black top and had no license plates. Only my mother was home. They tore up and broke everything, cutting open all the upholstery and mattresses, and tossing clothes and things in the middle of the floor. A few days after they ruined the house, a note was put under the door saying if we reported anything we would all be killed."

Alvarez, her children, and her mother moved to a new neighborhood. A few weeks later, a woman at the corner fruit stand said two men in a gray car with a black top had come around asking for her. The woman had pretended she didn't know who they were talking about. The following Sunday, Alvarez noticed two men following her in the market. A woman at the butcher's shop let her hide until the men went away.

"I left the children with my mother and hid with relatives, changing from one to another. For more than a year, I looked everywhere for my husband, going to morgues and hospitals. I would call the police about bodies and go to the morgues and look at them. I saw so many ugly things—battered, mutilated bodies—that it is like a nightmare in my mind. Finally, I believed that my husband had been killed and if I stayed to look any more, I would be killed too."

Alvarez went alone to Mexico City in the summer of 1983, evading roadblocks by hitching rides from truckers who hid her among the bananas and furniture they were carrying. She also got a ride from a man and woman in a camper. "They were gringos and treated me very well. The fat man wore a pistol, and when we stopped at a checkpoint he showed them an ID and spoke to them in English."

Through the help of a friend, Alvarez found a church in Mexico City and a priest, Father Paco, who was helping Central Americans. He gave her clothes, and, in early 1984, he helped her enroll in a school to learn how to use an industrial sewing machine. She had been attending classes for three days when, at a soda stand in front of the building, the *migra* got her.

"They asked for my papers.

" 'I don't have them with me.'

" 'How much *pisto* are you carrying?'

" 'I don't have any.'

" 'How many *patojos* [children] do you have?'

" 'I don't have any kids.'

" 'Cut the crap, we know you're Guatemalan. You're coming with us.'

"I didn't want to walk. They forced me around a corner to a parked car, where another two men waited. I started crying. They blindfolded me. We arrived at an uninhabited house where they tied me to a chair and said a lot of gross things to me. They started drinking. They took off the blindfold and tied it around my mouth. Then they untied me, three left the room, and the one who remained threw me on the bed, hit me, and raped me. They all raped me, then tied me to the chair. They raped me repeatedly over a period of three days. I bled a great deal. On the third day they took me to government headquarters in the middle of Mexico City."

At Gobernación, Alvarez was given cotton to staunch the bleeding and told that if she did not confess to being Guatemalan, she would be taken to the basement and tortured. "I was so afraid to be deported that I was still insisting I was a Mexican from Chiapas. They took me to a lawyer who said, 'Look, my child, tell them all the data about yourself so they won't take you down below. Better not to be beaten again, just to be deported anyway.' I was crying and begging that they not send me to Guatemala, but he said that it was their job and nothing could be done about it. So I told them my name and said I am Guatemalan. They sent me to an immigration prison."

Alvarez was very sick from the blood that had coagulated in her. A prison doctor told her to take up a collection from the other prisoners so she could get some pills. She did, and the other women gave her money, orange juice, and an overcoat. It was February, and Alvarez had a high fever.

"The bus trip to the border was rough. I cried in pain, and I don't know how I survived the trip. There was also a Salvadoran woman with a 10-day-old baby who had been delivered by Caesarian section. She showed us where they had cut her to deliver the baby. She suffered a great deal on the bus.

"They took us to Talisman. On the Guatemalan side, the Guatemalans were separated from the Salvadorans. The Guatemalans were interrogated and let go. The Salvadorans were detained. One of the Salvadoran women had helped me a lot and I was sad and worried, too, about the woman with the 10-day-old baby. She was in very bad condition."

Alvarez went to Coatepeque, where she found medical help and work in a diner. While there, she sent a telegram to her mother, who wrote back that suspicious men were still asking about her and it was not safe to return. Alvarez did not tell her mother she had been raped: "I don't want her to suffer any more because of me."

When she could travel again, Alvarez went to the border and hitched a ride to Mexico City in a tanker truck. She went to visit Father Paco and found he was being transferred to another church. "He said he had been ordered not to tell where he would be. I think he got in trouble for helping Central Americans too much." Alvarez learned about a church organization in Ajusco that helped Central Americans. From there she got 2,000 pesos [then, $10.50], some rice, beans, sugar, soap, and oil. The church workers said they would give her groceries every Wednesday for a month.

Alvarez, although still sick, went to work as a maid. She was living with an elderly couple when Corbett met her. "They are very good people and treat me like their daughter, but they don't want to get mixed up in my problems," she told Corbett. "I have not told them everything for fear they would be shocked and reject me. Most of the time I stay in the house. I'm afraid to go outside because the *migra* might catch me again, and if they recognized me they would probably do something even worse to me.

"It is very painful being separated from my children and not knowing what is happening at home. Sometimes I think death would be better than this kind of life."

Because Alvarez's story was never entered in evidence, it is unknown whether Judge Carroll knew what had happened to her when he wrote, "the record does not indicate that any of the aliens named in this indictment suffered an imminent threat to their lives or freedom immediately before entering the United States from Mexico." Circumstances like Alvarez's were not dire enough, in Carroll's opinion, to warrant a "necessity" defense.

The morning of December 10, the jury was excused so that Reno could demonstrate what he'd done to find Juana Alvarez since her escape. The prosecutor put Tucson border patrolman Willie Garcia on the stand, and Garcia described his efforts to locate Alvarez through the clinics where she'd received medical attention, the cleaning service where she'd worked, the post office, and the electric company. To no one's surprise, he'd come up empty—Carmen Duarte had reported in the *Star* that Alvarez had left town in July. Garcia's efforts were "a thorough attempt to revive some very stale leads," as Steve Cooper said. If the government had really wanted to find her, Corbett's lawyer argued, they would have followed up back in January. The judge had to agree. The next morning, Carroll ruled that the government had failed to show good faith in its search for Alvarez. He ordered suppressed anything Cruz might say about her.

Left without Alvarez's hearsay statements, Reno tried to enter into evidence a photo Ron Medvescek had taken of Corbett helping her through a barbed-wire fence. Apparently Reno had already discarded the idea of using Carmen Duarte's story, with its details of Alvarez's past. But Steve Cooper fought to keep the photo out. "We wanted to hold Reno to all or nothing," Corbett said. Cooper pointed out that the prosecutor was going to need a foundation witness—the photographer—to say that the picture was taken at the border, and not, say, in someone's backyard. Reno then announced he would subpoena Ron Medvescek.

Medvescek, a friend of Corbett's, had already decided he wasn't going to testify. The executive editor of the *Star* supported his decision and issued a statement saying the paper had no intention of cooperating with the government. Reno countered that he would attempt to get the Attorney General's approval to subpoena a member of the press. He must not have received it, because Medvescek was never served and the photo never entered. Reno ended by dropping all charges against Corbett except conspiracy.

JANUARY 15 AND 16, 1986

The prosecutor had an only slightly less difficult time proving the rest of his case. To corroborate what Cruz had said, he was forced to call a number of reluctant and uncooperative witnesses, the "illegal alien unindicted co-conspirators" who had been helped by the Tucson sanctuary groups to enter the country during 1984. The INS had already started deportation proceedings against these people and their families. They may have been compelled to testify, but they weren't going to make it easy on Reno.

Alejandro Rodríguez, a 44-year-old Salvadoran labor leader, was the first refugee witness to take the stand after the defense's three-week cross-examination of Cruz. Dressed in a dark, three-piece suit, his short, stocky frame pulled up, Rodríguez faced the prosecutor with a defiant look. Reno didn't get far before the Salvadoran made it clear whose side he was on. He refused to identify Father Quiñones, and when Reno asked if he'd stayed at Socorro Aguilar's, Rodríguez said, "She was the only person who offered me a roof over my head when I was most in need."

"How did you get to Mrs. Aguilar's house?"

"At the church, I was told there was a lady with a good heart who helped people. I remember her very well and with much love."

Rodríguez's testimony proceeded in this manner, with Reno repeatedly asking Judge Carroll to strike the Salvadoran's answers as unresponsive. When it came time for the defense to question Rodríguez, Reno was even busier, jumping up to object over and over again. The judge, who had cautioned the defense that "we're not going to get into ears and eyes and individual tortures," for the most part sustained Reno's objections.

Rodríguez described his life in El Salvador. He said he had been an industrial electrician and the production manager of the plant where he worked. His wife was comptroller for the Salvadoran subsidiary of an American company. They owned a bus that brought in an additional $100 a day, a farm, and two homes, one of which they rented. All together, they earned over $40,000 a year—clearly not "economic migrants." The family lost everything when they fled.

Rodríguez was secretary of a construction union that represented thousands of Salvadoran workers. For that, he said, he was jailed and tortured.

Reno objected. His assistant, Joan Grabowski, spoke Spanish, and she translated the witness's answers for him before the judge or the jury had heard the court interpreter's translation. The defense learned to ask questions in a euphemistic way: "Without going into details, did something terrible happen to you?" But any time a witness used the words "tortured" or "killed," Carroll had the answer stricken from the record.

Rodríguez went to the office of the U.N. High Commissioner for Refugees in Mexico City. He showed them a newspaper clipping that said he had been jailed by the Salvadoran government, and after a three-hour interview, the UNHCR gave him a letter designating him as a political refugee. Rodríguez waited for four months for the United States, Canada, Holland, Belgium, or Switzerland to admit him as a political refugee, but as time went by, he became increasingly impatient. At any moment, he and his family could have been arrested and deported. He decided to enter the United States "without inspection."

Rodríguez described the day he came through the fence. Cruz had suggested his children pass through with some Mexican youngsters playing at customs. "That didn't seem to me to be a very safe or sure idea," Rodríguez said. "My children aren't used to being out in the street. Mr. Cruz also offered to take us in a taxi. I thought that was very dangerous. In my country, taxi drivers are closely connected to the police.

"A woman there offered to take me and my two kids to another neighborhood. She dropped us off and we walked for about 15 minutes, looking for a hole in the fence to get in. We had a little trouble. One of the people who lived there offered to cross us. He wanted to charge me. I refused his offer, because I know there are people who make money on us. Then he said he was going to tell the police. I was very afraid. We walked faster to try to find a hole."

Rodríguez, his wife, and two older children found a hole, stepped through the fence, and walked to Sacred Heart. There, they were reunited with their two youngest, who had crossed the border in a van with other children. Two Anglo women (whom Rodríguez did not identify, and Cruz had said were Kay Kelly and Katherine Flaherty) drove the family to Tucson. The Rodríguezes spent several weeks traveling before they reached Rochester, New York, where they were now living in a Presbyterian Church.

Reno had brought out that Rodríguez didn't file for political asylum until after he was arrested, thus making it look as if he had only requested it to put off being deported. Defense lawyers tried to give Rodríguez the chance to explain why he'd waited.

"I needed time to gather documentation, and my attorney told me that only 2 to 3 percent of people from El Salvador—"

Reno jumped up, cutting off the answer. Rodríguez was not allowed to finish his sentence. Judge Carroll agreed with the prosecutor that the percentage of applications denied was irrelevant.

Rodríguez was done with his testimony in front of the jury, but defense lawyers still wanted him to "make a record" on the circumstances of his departure from El Salvador. Making a record meant that Rodríguez could tell his story for the trial record, even though Judge Carroll had ruled that the jury wouldn't hear it. An appeals court might overturn convictions on the grounds that Rodríguez's story was relevant, after all.

Rodríguez said that because of his union activities and membership in the Christian church, he was captured by the Salvadoran police, jailed, and tortured for 15 days and nights. He was hung from his arms and beaten. They hit him with hands, feet, wood, iron, and towels. They shocked him with a cattle prod. They threatened to kidnap his children and kill them if he didn't admit he was a guerrilla. Finally, after 23 days, he was transferred to the general prison. More than five hundred political prisoners were in the prison, nine to twelve per room and only three or four beds. He was fed a tablespoon of beans, a thin tortilla, and a cup of coffee three times a day. He was never charged with any crime and never tried.

After six months in prison, Rodríguez was released. He said it was because he knew a powerful factory owner who spoke to a military judge about his case. He was on his way home when he heard that a death squad was waiting for him. He hid at a friend's house and left the country that same night without even telling his wife. A few weeks later, with the help of friends, he was able to have his entire family leave the country as well. He took his family with him, he said, because "in El Salvador, they murder three-month-old babies. They rape girls that are five, six, seven years old. Their vengeance would or could have been their kidnapping, raping, or murdering my children."

The next afternoon, after Mrs. Rodríguez testified, the couple went back to Rochester. Four months later, Rodríguez was arrested again. This time the INS put a $50,000 bond on him, claiming he represented a national security risk. Officials wouldn't say why, but a Rochester newspaper speculated it was because Rodríguez had traveled to Cuba and the Soviet Union in the early 1960s. The Rochester sanctuary committee raised the money, but at the end of June, Rodríguez took his family and fled to Canada. He said he had lost faith in our legal system.

JANUARY 17 AND 18, 1986

After hearing only part of Rodríguez's story, one juror said later, she went home and cried all night. It seemed things couldn't get any worse for Reno, but they did. His next witness was a frightened 15-

year-old named Ana Benavides. She was a skinny girl with big eyes and long frizzy hair, wearing tight jeans and a black plastic jacket. With her face down, Ana said she and her brother Julio first left El Salvador in December 1983. They were going to Phoenix to be with their parents, whom they hadn't seen in five years. Accompanied by an aunt, the Benavides children traveled to Mexico City, to Hermosillo, and then to Nogales.

"Were you lodged in Nogales?" Reno asked.

"We weren't lodged, we. . . ." Benavides, who had been on the stand less than ten minutes, burst into tears.

Judge Carroll called a recess for the girl to collect herself. "Nice going, Don," Ellen Yaroshefsky snapped at Reno after the jurors filed out.

Benavides, her brother, and her aunt had been intercepted at the Benjamin Hill checkpoint. Later, James Brosnahan, Socorro Aguilar's attorney, explained "for the record" what had happened. A Mexican immigration officer had gotten on the bus and told Benavides's aunt that he knew a coyote who helped Central Americans. When she refused to talk to him, he told her that he knew who they were, and he would kill Julio and rape Ana if she still refused to talk. The aunt broke down and admitted they were Salvadoran. She was let go, and Ana and Julio were put in the Sonoran prison.

They were in jail for a month and a half. During that time, they were befriended by Socorro Aguilar and Father Quiñones. The two teenagers were eventually deported, but in May 1984, they tried again to make it to Phoenix. This time, Aguilar met them at the airport in Mexico City and took them with her to Nogales.

Prompted by Reno, Benavides said she'd been at Aguilar's a few days when Aguilar gave her a border-crossing card and told her to memorize the name on it. Aguilar put a scarf on the girl's head and rollers in her hair to make her look more like the woman in the photograph. Then Jesús Cruz drove them to the border, and Aguilar walked ahead of her through the turnstyle into the United States. (The guards at the gate had been tipped off by the INS that Aguilar and Benavides were coming through, and they let the girl pass with only a glance at the card. The defense considered this entrapment; the judge did not.)

Brosnahan asked Ana if Aguilar had arranged for her to talk to her brother and her parents when she was in jail. She had. Had Aguilar brought clothes, shoes, money, and a radio? Yes. She brought food that wasn't spicy? Yes. Did the food in jail cause your lips to be chapped?

Reno objected, Carroll sent the jury out, and that was the end of that line of questioning.

Ana Benavides was not the only witness to cry on the stand. The last Central American to testify, a Guatemalan named Miriam Hernández, broke down when Reno asked her if she had thanked Mr. Conger for his help. Hernández continued to cry while the jury was sent out, and then began hyperventilating, until Nena MacDonald was able to calm her. Outside the courtroom, Corbett commented that he had seen other instances in which a seemingly innocuous question or event pushed a refugee over the edge. "One woman I knew was hit by a car while she was riding her bicycle, not very hard, but when she fell off she was completely paralyzed for a while," Corbett said. "She wasn't making it up. It was a real, physical reaction."

In between Benavides and Hernández, eleven other Salvadorans and one Guatemalan gave moving testimony about their backgrounds. Almost every witness had had someone in their immediate family die violently. One young Salvadoran described his attempt to apply for political asylum at the U.S. embassy in San Salvador. He said the guard at the door told him unless he had $10,000, a house, or a car, he could forget it. Another witness, Guatemalan Joel Morelos, was deaf in one ear from the torture he had received. He managed to slip this information in when Reno asked him if he had overheard the defendants' conversation.

Salvadoran medical student Francisco Nieto-Núñez had worked in a refugee camp before being arrested. Nieto-Núñez was a small, quiet man who now lived with his family on the Rutgers University campus in New Jersey. He did not say this on the stand, but both he and his wife had experienced repeated torture by the Salvadoran military. His wife had been sexually tortured in front of him, and soldiers had also held his infant son's head under water while Nieto-Núñez watched to make him confess to being a guerrilla. After twenty-seven days of torture and eleven months in Mariona prison, Nieto-Núñez won his release by bribing a judge. He then fled the country with his family. He told the jury that INS agent John Nixon had threatened to send him back to El Salvador unless he came to Tucson to testify against the sanctuary workers.

Reno had a great deal of trouble with these hostile witnesses. "Why is it they can remember every detail of their alleged experiences in their countries, but they can't remember anything about how they entered the United States?" he asked in frustration. In his closing statement, he called it the "sanctuary *no recuerdo* memory-lapse syndrome." ("*No recuerdo*" means "I don't remember" in Spanish.) The prosecutor was also annoyed by the defense lawyers' constant barrage of prejudicial and inflammatory questions, and he urged Judge Carroll to hold them in contempt.

Carroll refrained from holding any attorneys in contempt, but, in his own way, he contained the defense. He sustained Reno's objections or even raised an objection himself when he thought a question was inappropriate. His scowls and grimaces indicated obvious disapproval, and he sent the jury out of the room whenever he felt an attorney needed particular admonishment. All of this led the defense to believe that Carroll was, in the words of Robert Hirsh, "the quintessential biased judge." Corbett called the judge a neo-Hobbesian; "He really sees himself as the law. He thinks, 'If I am not obeyed, the law is coming apart.'"

FEBRUARY 2, 1986

Southeastern Arizona is a rugged, grassy region with miles of border fence running across remote canyons and mountains. Jim Corbett knew the area well, having ranched with his family in the Huachuca Mountains for many years, and he considered it a good place to smuggle people into the country. In March 1985, Corbett showed Tucson refugee workers a new route, through Coronado National Monument, a park that touched the border 40 miles east of Nogales. It soon became a favorite crossing place.

The sky over Coronado National Monument was clear and cold this Sunday afternoon in February. Seven Americans, posing as picnickers and birdwatchers, loitered by a rusted windmill and dry water tank, waiting for their counterparts in Mexico to bring two Salvadoran families up to the fence. One family were catechists who had lost several members to the Salvadoran army; the other had been targeted by the guerrillas because the father (now dead) and several other family members belonged to ORDEN, the civilian paramilitary organization that was the "eyes" and "fingers" of the National Guard. Both families had been screened by the Tucson refugee support group and were found to be deserving of aid.

A little after 4:00, refugees and sanctuary workers appeared on the other side of the fence. Seven Salvadorans were helped through the strands of barbed wire, and then the whole group starting walking the mile up to the road. They kept a sharp ear out for an approaching plane or car. Sound traveled for miles in the empty canyon, and they could hear the wind long before they felt it or saw it move the trees.

The border-breakers reached their cars. Using a procedure Corbett had devised, the Anglo sanctuary workers rode in front, the Salvadorans rode in back, and each driver left five minutes apart. Barry Lazarus, the jeweler who was renting Corbett's old refugee-apartment, drove a car with the woman who had belonged to ORDEN, and her two school-age sons. He waited for two other cars to leave and then started up the mountain. A fourth car, carrying several more sanctuary workers and the catechist-refugees, stayed behind to wait.

At the top of the mountain, the driver of the first car stopped to adjust the car seats for the two infants she was carrying. The second car caught up to her, and by the time they started down the mountain, Lazarus was right behind them. The three cars reached the bottom of the mountain, passed the ranger station, and headed toward the highway. Lazarus realized they were too close together. Right at that moment, he said, "I looked down this wide open plain between the United States and Mexico. About a half-mile away, out on the main highway, I saw a green Border Patrol car. I knew then we were burnt."

As the border patrolmen went around the corner, they looked over the occupants of the three cars waiting to turn on to the highway. The driver said something to his partner, and then leaned out the window and shouted "Pull over!" The sanctuary workers started up the highway as if they hadn't heard. The Border Patrol swung around and came after them, waving each one over in turn.

Saying nothing, Lazarus gave the two patrolmen a letter that Jim Corbett had written and sent along with the group. The letter was addressed to Ruth Anne Myers, and explained that these Salvadorans, whom Corbett listed by name, were in transit to Canada. Corbett asked the INS to allow them to stay temporarily in the United States. The border patrolmen were unimpressed. One glanced over the letter and said, "You people are messing with my children's future."

At Naco, a tiny border town about 12 miles away, the Border Patrol occupied an ornate, Spanish-style building with wooden scrollwork framing the doors. The sanctuary workers and Salvadorans were taken there and held until well past dark. Lazarus tried to call Corbett, but there was no answer. Someone else called Bates Butler, who advised them to say nothing. After several hours, their cars confiscated, the sanctuary workers and refugees were driven to Tucson in two Border Patrol cars.

In a converted mobile home in south Tucson, the Americans were separated from the Salvadorans, and the men from the women. Lazarus and an older man named Cliff Pine were put in a small cubicle. The three women in the next cubicle kept their spirits up by praying and singing religious songs. At 10 o'clock, a border patrolman came around with a bag of hamburgers, but no one was hungry. Lazarus went to the bathroom, but he couldn't urinate. Someone finally came in and searched them. According to Pine, the border patrolman's eyes lit up when he saw a small square bulging in the corner of Pine's wallet. He seemed to think he'd found drugs. When the patrolman saw it was a hearing aid, Pine said, his face fell. Lazarus had a few pieces of paper with phone numbers that were taken. Then the five sanctuary workers were fingerprinted and photographed, and led back to their cubicles.

At 1:00 A.M., the sanctuary workers were called in individually and told they were being released on their own recognizance. The Salvadorans, still silent, were taken to a detention center outside Las Vegas. The TEC bonded them out several days later.

News of the arrest traveled fast. The next day, some of the defendants and lawyers met with the "Naco Five," as they came to be called. Corbett said he was taken to task for writing the letter. "The lawyers' feeling was, 'This'll hurt the trial. We don't want the jury to know this is still going on.'" Corbett was unperturbed. After the indictment, the lawyers had also tried to stop the defendants from publicly announcing that sanctuary work would continue. "They want me to crawl into a hole until the trial is over, and I'm not going to," Corbett said.

Pat Corbett was concerned that Reno might use her husband's involvement with the arrest to get him jailed for the rest of the trial. But Reno didn't mention it, and by Wednesday it was apparent the incident was not going to come up in court. The lawyers dissuaded the Naco Five from making a public statement, and the government decided not to press charges against them. Although officials did not say why, sanctuary workers speculated the case was dropped for the same reason that charges against Phil Willis-Conger were dismissed in 1984: the Border Patrol had had no probable cause to make the stop.

This incident created more controversy within the movement than with the government. The news that Corbett was helping ORDEN members caused a ripple in the Tucson community and refueled the debate with the Chicago Religious Task Force that had been simmering since the symposium. Several defendants felt that Corbett should refrain from writing letters for questionable refugees while on trial with people who didn't necessarily share his views. They said this was one more example of Corbett's maverick style, his acting alone without consulting anyone else first. People in other parts of the country were upset to hear that the Tucson group was helping death-squad members. Corbett explained that these refugees met Tucson refugee support group guidelines, and, in any case, merely attending ORDEN meetings, as the young woman was reputed to have done, was no reason to refuse her aid.

"ORDEN was organized to get peasants on the side of the government," Corbett said, "so in addition to being involved in death-squad activity, it's something like the VFW, or the Knights of Columbus. And it has definite advantages for those who belong. They don't get murdered when they're stopped at roadblocks." (The woman's brother was spared at a roadblock where several other young men on the bus with him were killed.) "The family was definitely targeted for being known members of ORDEN. They had reason to think poisoned milk was delivered to the house. The father was hacked apart, and another family member was gang-raped. She was not with the others when they arrived because she was still in Mexico, giving birth to the child of that rape.

"Whatever the family's involvement in ORDEN," Corbett concluded, "a young woman in a right-wing organization in El Salvador doesn't go around in the middle of the night killing people."

Corbett pointed out that the family of catechists who made it through, and who had experienced tortures and disappearances by the military, became close friends with the ORDEN-connected family during their trip from El Salvador. "A lot of these doctrinaire notions of what it means to belong to ORDEN, or how people line up politically, are not very accurate indicators of reality," Corbett said. "People join something like ORDEN for a lot of reasons, and people who travel and risk things together have personal likes and dislikes that bond them, regardless of their ideological outlook."

The Chicago Task Force maintained that because sanctuary was a movement for refugees, it should do what the refugees want, and not what Anglo sanctuary workers thought was good policy. "Many refugees have had their families killed by ORDEN," Sister Nicgorski said at the trial. The Chicago task force didn't see how filling U.S. churches with "*contras* and ORDEN members" served the cause of ending wars in Central America. "What is the value of a sanctuary church that continues its support (by silence, by vote or whatever) for U.S. policies in Central America?" wrote Chicago in the January 1985 *Basta!*. "We see little benefit in a sanctuary movement that is a mile wide and an inch deep."

In their book, Renny Golden and Michael McConnell character-ized the Tucson-Chicago debate as "charity versus liberation." They chastised American liberals who "believe there is a middle ground in national and international power conflicts," and who "blame victims for their 'excesses.'" The Chicago position was grounded in libera-tion theology and the Catholic "just war" doctrine, which acknowl-edged that people will eventually take up arms against a dictatorial government that is killing them, either through violence or neglect. "There is a limit to the number of times a people can bear walking a tiny coffin to some remote graveyard," the Chicago task force wrote.

Corbett didn't deny that these situations existed in the world, nor did he claim to preach nonviolence to those people. His moral phi-losophy was based on his position in life: He was a white man who grew up in a country where there was plenty of land and all points of view were tolerated, as long as no one resorted to violence. Like most Americans, Corbett believed in this kind of life for everyone, and he wanted a speedy end to the suffering in Central America.

The question was how one "fought for democracy," or created a just society in countries that had known only corruption and exploitation for centuries. Quakers understood that wars rarely created just societies, because the side that won was usually the side willing to stop at nothing to gain control. Too often, a fascist government of the right was replaced by a fascist government of the left. Quakers maintained that with demilitarization and self-determination, small nations were capable of establishing representative governments. Unfortunately, by its military support of right-wing governments in Central America, the United States had never given democracy a chance. Salvadorans and Americans attempting to institute the agrarian-reform program had been murdered, with slight protest from the United States. The U.S. government ignored the efforts of the Contadora nations (Mexico, Panama, Venezuela, and Colombia) to achieve a negotiated settlement to the *contra* war in Nicaragua and an end to the infusion of weapons to Central America from other countries. The deaths of many thousands would continue until the United States agreed to an overhaul of the military apparatuses of Guatemala and El Salvador and the perpetrators of war crimes in those countries were brought to justice. Argentina was one nation in this hemisphere that had begun to come to terms with the murderous excesses of its recent past. But the poor countries of Central America were, as the old joke about Mexico said, "so far from God and so close to the United States."

Because he wouldn't advocate violence in the name of peace, Corbett had to be content to take a long-term view. He recognized that he was open to charges of appeasement and collaboration from both sides. William Penn had said Quakers, above all others, must be willing to stand in the gap, and that meant even in a polarized situation such as El Salvador's. Corbett described the difference between his position and Chicago's this way:

There is a faith that is primarily belief. This kind of faith calls for definitive doctrines from which guiding objectives and priorities can be derived. And there is a faith that is primarily trust. This kind of faith expects to be guided by a unifying presence that enlivens each moment, breaks all borders, gathers us into communion with one another, and addresses us in all we meet. For faith as belief, it makes sense to ask how all we presently encounter can be used to achieve our (or God's) objectives; the present must be sacrificed to the future. For faith as trust, the future we hope for must emerge out of a fulfilled present; to treat any being or situation we meet only as means to be used or as an obstacle to be eliminated attacks the historically unique liberating power with which every person and every community is endowed.

Corbett had also described this as the difference between a world view that sees good and evil locked in an eternal struggle for domination, and one that sees both good and evil as part of the creation.

The church had argued over the use of violence for seventeen centuries. So, as Corbett said, the debate was unlikely to be resolved by the sanctuary movement. The Chicago task force was dismayed by the media fascination with the controversy. Corbett, however, refused to shut up. As a Quaker, he didn't believe in the kind of unity that squelched minority viewpoints, and he also felt it more important to say what he thought than to present a united front. He felt the debate may even have strengthened the movement. Gandhi said, "Truth never damages a cause that is just."

FEBRUARY 4, 1986

Not all of Reno's Central American witnesses were hostile to him. Several, in fact, were distinctly hostile to the defense. These pro-government Salvadorans were all relatives or friends of Bertha Benavides and Cecilia de Emory—the two women who had pleaded guilty to a lesser charge and were dropped from the indictment shortly after it was announced. None of this group had been screened or approved for aid by the Tucson sanctuary organizations, and Corbett suspected they had been recruited by the government to set up the sanctuary workers.

Mrs. Benavides began sending her extended family to Father Quiñones and Socorro Aguilar in May 1984, a few weeks after they helped reunite her with her two teenage children, Ana and Julio. She also sent, via Cruz, two $100 checks as "alms" for the church. (This was the money that Reno had characterized as payment for services rendered, until the defense pointed out that he couldn't argue motive.) Father Quiñones and Socorro helped the Benavides's relations get across to Sacred Heart, where they met up with Cruz and he drove them to Phoenix. Cruz usually stopped at Southside Church on the way, to introduce the Salvadorans to Fife or Willis-Conger or whoever happened to be there. After a couple of months, Aguilar and Father Quiñones caught on that they were being used, and they told Cruz to stay away from Mrs. Benavides. By then it was too late.

José René Argueta, a 45-year-old man with a crew-cut, was the most outspoken of the pro-government witnesses. In contrast to the "Sí" and "No" responses of other refugees, Argueta volunteered a great deal of information. He described in elaborate detail how Father Quiñones gave him the border-crossing card of a dead priest and Socorro Aguilar's daughter took him to buy priest's clothes. Argueta also insisted he'd come to the United States to get a job. "The unemployment situation is very critical in my country," he said.

Since Argueta brought it up, the defense took the opportunity to ask him just what the situation was in his country. This was the first time in the trial that Judge Carroll allowed extensive questioning about Central America. Argueta, who now lived with his wife in Hampstead, Long Island, and worked at a chocolate-milk factory, was originally from San Miguel, El Salvador. His mother and four of his five children still lived there.

"Mr. Argueta, is there a war going on in El Salvador?"

"Everyone knows that."

"Was it going on when you left?"

"In a peaceful way."

"Was there danger to civilians?"

"Not that I know of. I used to just devote myself to my work. I was not paying attention to other situations in the country."

"Were civilian centers being bombed?"

"Perhaps, perhaps not."

"Was there forced recruitment into the military?"

Reno objected, but he was overruled.

"Not that I was aware of."

"If a man is recruited and refuses to serve, is he subject to violence?"

"I don't know. I've had no experience with that."

"Have you ever been in the military?"

"No." Neither Argueta nor his 22-year-old son, who now lived in Brooklyn, had served in the Salvadoran army.

"You don't know what happens to the families of men who refuse to serve?"

"No."

"Did you tell Father Quiñones you were afraid you'd be killed because you hadn't served?"

"I swear before God I didn't say that."

"Did you tell him you left for political reasons?"

"No, I didn't."

Argueta's claim that he was rarely stopped at roadblocks in El Salvador, even though he used to commute by private car two hours a day, indicated to Jim Corbett that he might have belonged to a right-wing party. Argueta said he never saw any fighting in San Miguel, he had never heard of death squads, and he actually wanted to go home right away. "I could return tomorrow and my town is at peace," he said.

Argueta's testimony was directly contradicted by two young men, also from San Miguel, who followed him on the stand. One said the army had mobilized all "young people—between the ages of 13 and 45" there. Another revealed that, unlike Argueta, he *was* going back to El Salvador the next day. Silver Isaac Palacios, a curly-haired man in his early twenties, appeared so terrified at the prospect that he could barely talk. He sat frozen, staring straight ahead. ("At first we thought he was stoned," said a juror. With the jury excused, Reno said he thought Palacios was feigning forgetfulness.) Palacios explained under cross-examination that he'd signed a voluntary departure order and was already on the plane, when Rayburn got on and brought him back to testify. Judge Carroll allowed defense attorneys to ask Palacios the same questions they'd asked Argueta, and the young man gave a very different picture of his hometown. He described it as a war zone, with the electricity frequently cut off, roads blocked, and bus service halted. Sounds of fighting could be heard all over the city. Bombs dropped near his house. Bates Butler asked if he'd seen bodies in the streets, a question the defense had tried to ask before, without success. This time, Carroll allowed it.

"Why do you ask me that? That affects me a great deal. My family is still living there." Palacios's voice dropped to nothing.

"I appreciate that. I just need to know whether or not you saw bodies in the streets where you were living?"

"Yes."

FEBRUARY 19, 1986

As he neared the end of his case, Reno grew increasingly concerned the jury might acquit. His star witness's credibility had been badly shaken, and the defense was able to get in much more prejudicial and inflammatory testimony than he would have liked. He asked Judge Carroll to strike all the testimony about conditions in Central America, but Carroll refused. Needing to corroborate Cruz on every count, he decided to subpoena four more witnesses: three "unindicted co-conspirators" and one more "illegal alien unindicted co-conspirator."

Kay Kelly, Tucson Methodist minister George Lockwood, and Mary Ann Lundy, a Presbyterian elder who had worked with refugees at Riverside Church in New York City, were the only American sanctuary supporters whom Reno tried to put on the stand. Their response was predictable—they all refused to testify. This, added to all the other problems he'd had with witnesses, made Reno mad. He accused the defense of deliberately trying to "break down and confuse this prosecution." He urged Judge Carroll to make the sanctuary workers "pay the price" for refusing.

Judge Carroll ignored Reno's urging. He decided instead to place the three under house arrest, with orders not to leave their homes, except in case of a life-or-death emergency, or to attend church once a week, until the end of the trial. Kelly, Lockwood, and Lundy were very relieved. "It was a well-balanced move, politically," Corbett said. "He managed to pull the sting, both in terms of public reaction and the state's seeming to be heavy-handed."

Elba Teresa Lopez, the only Salvadoran called by Reno to refuse to take the stand, came before the court the next day. Lopez had a different reason for declining to testify than the three American-citizen sanctuary workers, who had cited their First Amendment right to freedom of religion. Lopez said it was her fear of what might happen to her family, or her, should she be deported after news of her testimony was disclosed in El Salvador. Judge Carroll offered to exclude the press. But it wasn't the press she was afraid of.

"Without impugning Mr. Reno in any way," Katrina Pflaumer, Lopez's lawyer, explained, "she believes there is a transfer of information between the INS and the government of El Salvador."

Lopez had good reason to believe that. The family of another witness, Joel Morelos, had already suffered because of Morelos's involvement with the case. In October, the apartment in which Morelos and his wife were living was broken into, and papers with addresses on them were taken. Morelos was arrested in January, and on February 2 his brother and cousin were tortured and killed in Guatemala. A few months later, Morelos received a letter, mailed from Philadelphia, to a New York address known only to his family in Guatemala. It contained clippings from a Guatemalan newspaper announcing the kidnapping, torture, and murder of his brother and cousin. In *No Promised Land*, Gary MacEoin and Nivita Riley reported on the case of Ana Estela Guevara-Flores, who was arrested by the INS in San Antonio, Texas, in June 1981. Agents found letters from Salvadoran church officials in her possession, and accused her of being a well-known guerrilla, "Commandante Norma." She wasn't, but the FBI asked the Salvadoran government to investigate, and Guevara-Flores's sister and elderly mother were arrested and tortured.

Judge Carroll decided that Lopez's fear of foreign prosecution was not well grounded, and he scheduled her contempt hearing for the afternoon. Lopez's two young children sat in the front row while Lopez and her lawyer went before the judge. The jury was absent, never learning that these four witnesses had refused to testify.

Judge Carroll had a few questions about the documentation Lopez's lawyer had provided. He asked about a newspaper clipping from Seattle, which implied Lopez was selling photos for a $10 donation to University Baptist Church for a legal defense fund. Judge Carroll wanted to know if Lopez had been talking to the press.

Pflaumer explained that Pilar, Lopez's sister, was in public sanctuary at that Baptist Church, where she spoke to the press and church groups. Lopez, however, was gravely afraid and hadn't discussed her situation with anybody.

"It is hard to explain our system of separation of powers," Pflaumer went on, "that the court system can stand between an individual and the government. That is not so in El Salvador. She has no experiential base and can't cross that gulf. I'm hard put to explain the concept of a State Department leak."

"Does that give everyone who comes from a foreign country an excuse not to cooperate and comply with our laws?," Judge Carroll asked. "She came here voluntarily, and she must accept that the law is different here. We're dealing with a different system."

"I can understand that, but she can't." Pflaumer showed the judge drawings, done by Lopez's nephew, of bombs dropping on houses and soldiers beating and shooting prisoners. Carroll looked at the drawings in silence.

"It's hard for her to understand when the government has told her, 'We know you came for a job. You have nothing to fear and you should go back there,'" Pflaumer said as she took the pictures back.

Carroll said he thought that since people were speaking in churches on these matters, it would be easy enough to find them, if "someone"—presumably meaning the Salvadoran security forces —wanted to. "Now, whether putting these people on display does or doesn't affect them," he muttered, then interrupted himself, "I believe in our system. It's kept us going for over 200 years. It may fall down on occasion, but that doesn't justify people not following the law."

Carroll was voicing a common criticism of sanctuary. In 1984, Laura Dietrich, deputy assistant secretary of state for human rights and humanitarian affairs, stated it more explicitly when she told Dale Maharidge of the *Sacramento Bee* that she resented the sanctuary workers "using illegal aliens to influence foreign policy." Bill Johnston, head of the Tucson INS office, said he considered them little better than coyotes.

The phrases "putting people on display" and "using illegal aliens" implied that sanctuary was exploiting human beings for political purposes. Some conservative Christians also expressed reservations about parading refugees in front of cameras; they said they could understand helping people quietly, but, by going public, the movement crossed the line from religion to politics. "We thought about that," John Fife said. "Then we realized, by keeping it quiet, we were only helping the government cover up what was happening." To the charge that they were using people, sanctuary workers responded: We are saving lives. What is the government doing?

Judge Carroll sentenced Elba Teresa Lopez to house arrest. A year and a half later, Lopez's political asylum request was denied, and she and her children were ordered deported.

FEBRUARY 28, 1986

John Lafayette Nixon, Jr., Reno's final witness, was the only government agent and the only American citizen to testify. Since he was also the only witness who spoke English, his testimony proceeded much faster than that of the previous sixteen. Nixon gave a personal and anecdotal portrait of the defendants, recounting several arguments over whether certain refugees should be helped. Apparently he wanted to rebut the defense's portrayal of sanctuary workers as saintly do-gooders. At one point, he said, Fife asked him to cooperate with John Herzfeld, a Hollywood writer who was in town researching the sanctuary movement. "Rev. Fife said he's writing a movie about all this—and I quote—'bullshit.'"

Defense lawyers grilled Nixon, trying to make him look bad. Hirsh asked him if he knew anything about sanctuary workers visiting people in prison, about the Tucson Ecumenical Council, or about Archbishop Romero. Nixon said no. The agent said he had no interest in the defendants' backgrounds or religious affiliations. He even said he doubted Sister Nicgorski was a nun.

"Didn't you go to her alleged order to find out if she was a true nun or a fake nun?" Hirsh asked.

"No."

"She told you about her experiences in Guatemala, that her pastor was killed."

"Yes."

"About the suffering of the Guatemalan people?"

"I don't recall."

"That's not something you care about?"

"No, sir."

Sister Nicgorski was singled out by the government throughout the trial as somehow less sincere than the other defendants. Evidently this was because of her connection to the Chicago Religious Task Force, the perceived "political directors" of the movement. INS agents who searched Sister Nicgorski's apartment in Phoenix on the day of the indictment announced they'd found a file marked "terrorism." (The file contained clippings on right-wing terrorism in El Salvador and Guatemala, not evidence connecting sanctuary with left-wing terrorism.) Prior to sentencing, Reno told the judge that he had an FBI file on Sister Nicgorski, as well as a picture of her with "communist guerrillas down in Central America." The prosecutor turned down defense requests to look at Sister Nicgorski's FBI file, claiming it was classified.

Although government files on sanctuary and other Central American solidarity groups were secret, officials openly claimed that sanctuary helped communist terrorists to enter the United States. "INS documents requesting permission from the Justice Department to infiltrate the sanctuary movement in 1984 show that it was believed the 'aliens trafficked in are potential terrorists,'" wrote reporter Daniel Browning in the *Arizona Daily Star* on May 3, 1986. Don Reno told Browning that, given the opportunity, "I believe that I could prove beyond a reasonable doubt something more than the fact that they were smuggling aliens in."

Corbett scoffed at the communist label. "The reddest thing about me is my neck," he said. For others, particularly those outside the borders of the United States, the matter of government accusations was far more serious. Former Secretary of State Alexander Haig and former U.N. ambassador Jeane Kirkpatrick had first offered the picture of nuns with guns under their habits as an explanation for why four American church women were killed by Salvadoran national guardsmen in 1980. "The nuns were not just nuns," Kirkpatrick told the *Tampa Tribune* on December 16, 1980. "They were political activists on behalf of the *frente* [the FMLN, the leftist coalition battling El Salvador's government], and somebody who is using violence to oppose the *frente* killed those nuns." "Perhaps the vehicle that the nuns were riding in may have tried to run a roadblock or may have accidentally been perceived to have been doing so, and there may have been an exchange of fire," Haig told the House Foreign Affairs Committee in 1981. In fact, the women were taken to a remote location, raped, and then shot at close range in the back of the head.

No evidence connecting sanctuary with violent activities ever surfaced. Evidence that did come out pointed to just the opposite: that the U.S. government was intimately connected with Salvadoran death squads. Frank Varelli, the FBI informant who filed suit against his former employer in early 1987, said in his affidavit that he had been sent to El Salvador to make contact with the National Guard, people he knew to be death-squad members. (While there, Varelli was given a copy of the death squad's assassination list, which he

included in the papers filed with the court.) Varelli said he regularly
provided to Salvadoran national guardsmen the names of Salvadorans deported from the United States, as well as names of Americans
opposed to the administration's Central America policy who were
visiting El Salvador. Varelli also spent a great deal of time making
up a "Terrorist Photograph Album," which included photos and
descriptions of such noted "terrorists" as Senators Claiborne Pell,
Christopher Dodd, Congressman Michael Barnes, the Carter administration's ambassador to El Salvador Robert White (a vigor-
ous critic of current U.S. policy in that country), the Bishop of the
Catholic Diocese of Cuernavaca, Mexico, Sergio Mendez Arceo, and
Salvadoran Archbishop Arturo Rivera y Damas.

MARCH 14, 1986

High clouds swirled in the overcast sky, blown by winds across
the valley, on the day the defense was to begin presenting its case.
Winter had turned to spring, and the trial was entering its fifth
month. As the jury filed in to the courtroom this morning, they were
ready, some said later, to hear the other side of the story. Defense
lawyers had told everyone that James Rayburn was going to be their
first witness, and he was on the stand now. "Let's proceed," Judge
Carroll said.

Hirsh stood up. "As far as my case is concerned, Reverend Fife is
going to rest, your honor." Hirsh sat down.

"All right, fine," Carroll said.

Brosnahan then stood. "If the court please, on behalf of Mrs.
Socorro Aguilar, we rest." He sat down.

Ellen Yaroshefsky stood. "On behalf of Wendy LeWin, we rest."

They went around the table, each lawyer standing in turn and
resting on behalf of his or her client. Father Clark's attorney, William
Walker, went last. "Father Anthony Clark and the sanctuary defense
rests, your honor," Walker said, and sat down.

"What is the sanctuary defense? They are not a defendant in this
case, Mr. Walker."

With that retort, Carroll stole much of the defense's thunder.
He turned to the jury, told them that he had not known until this
moment what the defense was going to do, and then excused them.
The jurors were mystified. "Some of us wanted an instant replay,"

said one. Reno, too, was surprised. He said later he felt like an athlete who had prepared months for a competition, and, on the day of the event, his opponent failed to show up. Judge Carroll arranged to meet with the lawyers to discuss jury instructions and was about to leave the bench when Ellen Yaroshefsky asked if the witnesses under house arrest could now be let go.

"I'll review the matter," he said. Carroll did let them go, several days later.

After resting their case, the defendants and lawyers walked to the sanctuary defense fund media office for a press conference. Everyone was in high spirits. In one minute, they had moved the trial almost to its conclusion.

The lawyers said they had not decided until the night before to rest, but, once they did, they all agreed it was the right thing to do. They couldn't see the purpose of another round of battles with the judge. Carroll had already made it clear that he would not allow them to present their case.

At the same time, the defense appeared confident that the prosecutor had failed to make his case. "When you're ahead twenty-seven to nothing, why play the final quarter?" joked Michael Piccarreta, Peggy Hutchison's lawyer. "Reno wouldn't throw in the towel, so we threw it in for him."

Not only had the government failed in its burden of proof, the lawyers said, the jury had figured out what was going on. How, after hearing the refugees' testimony, could they not see the compelling necessity of the defendants' actions? Bates Butler commented that he thought the jury had also realized this was a case of selective prosecution. "If you take the $2 million it cost the government to put on this charade, hire all those Border Patrol agents—it's obvious that it was not for law-enforcement purposes," he said. (The trial finally cost the government $1.2 million, and the sanctuary defense funds just over $1 million, according to the *Arizona Daily Star*.)

Defense lawyers were correct in assuming that the jury had been moved by the refugees' testimony, but they overestimated the jurors' ability to look at the larger picture. The jury had almost no prior knowledge of sanctuary, avoided all media accounts of the trial, and spent most of the proceedings in the jury room. Several said afterwards they felt they had gotten only pieces of a puzzle. The jurors may also have had the perception that defense lawyers ought to do *something* on behalf of their clients.

The lawyers didn't say this to reporters in the media office, but they knew they had nothing to gain and a lot to lose by putting their clients on the stand. It would give Reno a chance to prove a number of counts he hadn't been able to prove so far. For their part, the defendants were reluctant to testify because they would not be allowed to tell the whole truth.

"The Bible says, when there is no opportunity to speak for the truth, then stand silent," Fife said.

"Whatever fragments of the truth permitted us would just be the structuring of a lie," Corbett said. Personally, Corbett was also concerned about having to "affirm" to tell the truth. (Quakers refused to "swear," because to do so implied one didn't always tell the truth.) "It created quite a problem for me," Corbett said. "I thought, how on earth can I do that? If I had to, I might have said, 'Yes, insofar as I am allowed.'"

The lawyers stood back while the defendants took seats in front of the television cameras and microphones. "We are happy and firm in having taken the decision to rest our defense," Father Quiñones said, his eyes twinkling in the hot lights. "Especially with the sure knowledge that the government took care of our defense. The government has shown, even with the lies of Jesús Cruz, that the vocation of the church of Christ has been expressed. We know the jury is made out of people who love justice and the truth. We can expect a just verdict, because it will be a verdict for history."

The following Wednesday, the lawyers met in Judge Carroll's courtroom in Phoenix to argue over jury instructions. The defense expected Carroll to give instructions consistent with his pretrial rulings, and they were not disappointed.

The judge's "mistake of law" instruction ruled out any possibility that the defendants acted legally. "A belief that an alien was a 'refugee' and was entitled to enter the United States without presentment, a mistake of law, does not negate the requisite state of mind," it said. Other instructions said that any noncitizen not duly admitted by an immigration officer is an illegal alien, and the mere possibility that an alien can file an asylum application after his entry does not entitle that person to enter or reside here legally. In other words, there was no way the defendants could win acquittal on the grounds that the Central Americans were political refugees.

Carroll turned down without comment the defense's proposed instructions on international law, the 1980 Refugee Act, necessity, and jury nullification. The defense also wanted a "humanitarian exception" included in the instruction on transporting, because, they argued, taking someone to a hospital (as Wendy LeWin had done for Miriam Hernández), was not in furtherance of the alien's illegal presence. Reno disagreed, saying the law afforded no such exception.

"Are you saying," Judge Carroll asked, "that if someone is driving down the highway and finds someone who says, 'I am here from El Salvador illegally and I have had a heart attack, will you take me to a hospital?' that they could be prosecuted for violating the law?"

"Well," Reno said, "under that hypothetical, your honor, I can't imagine a prosecutor that would seek an indictment under those facts, and if those were the facts—"

"Assuming there were such a hardhearted prosecutor in Pecos County, are you saying they can do that?" Carroll asked.

"We may dig one up in Maricopa," Piccarreta interjected, referring to the county that encompassed Phoenix.

"There is no law, your honor, that says that would not be in furtherance," Reno said. No humanitarian exception was included in the instructions.

Since Carroll had already included a "mistake of law" instruction, a major argument arose over the instruction on motive. Reno insisted on it. He said it went to the heart of his case, because the defense had elicited so much prejudicial and inflammatory testimony from the Rodríguezes, Joel Morelos, the Nieto-Núñezes— indeed, every witness except Argueta—that an instruction on motive was needed "to straighten the misleading and confusing state of the record as the jury now perceives it." For their part, the defense knew that specifically ruling motive out would be worse that omitting to mention it. They argued that such an instruction was unnecessary, since they hadn't been allowed to present any evidence on motive.

"The record is replete with evidence of motive," Reno protested. "This instruction is sorely needed in this case to do justice to the government and the law."

Carroll agreed and wrote the following instruction:

Intent and motive should never be confused. Motive is that which prompts a person to act. Intent refers to the state of mind with which an act is done.

Personal advancement, financial gain, political reason, religious beliefs, moral convictions, or some adherence to a higher law—even of nations— are well-recognized motives of human conduct. These motives may prompt one person to voluntary acts of good and another to voluntary acts of crime. Good motive is not a defense to intentional acts of crime.

So, if you find beyond a reasonable doubt that the acts constituting the crime charged were committed with the intent to commit the unlawful act and bring about the prohibited result, then the requirement that the act be done knowingly or willfully as defined in these instructions has been satisfied, even though the defendant may have believed that his conduct was politically, religiously, or morally required, or that ultimate good would result from such conduct.

Despite this devastating instruction, defense lawyers still ap-peared confident. "I usually pick them pretty well, and I thought there was no way they'd convict," Hirsh said. Pat Corbett was less optimistic. "I knew the judge had used the pretrial rulings and jury instructions to nail the defendants to the floor for the prosecution to walk on," she said.

APRIL 15, 1986

The jury instructions so supported the government's position that Reno spent much of his closing argument quoting them. He read the entire instruction on motive and told the jury that the supreme law of the land was made in Congress, not Southside Church. Even if the law appeared unfair, it must be followed. "During cross-exam-ination, you heard a lot about conditions in El Salvador, and about someone applying for political asylum a year after he gets here," Reno said. "But these things do not make an illegal entry legal."

Hirsh went first with his closing statement, and, as with the openings, he took the brunt of the judge's ire. He compared telling refugees to lie to the INS to "telling Jews in Nazi Germany to tell the Gestapo they're Catholic. Anybody who has a bit of humanity, or decency, would tell Central Americans to say they're Mexican." Carroll later reprimanded the lawyer for violating his ruling on the "necessity" defense.

Brosnahan, Yaroshefsky, and several other lawyers made their

closings with few interruptions. Then William Risner, Father Quiñones's attorney, tried to tell the jury how the "Brown Virgin" of
Guadalupe became Mexico's patron saint. Judge Carroll sent the
jury out and forbade Risner from mentioning the Virgin of Guadalupe again. Her story was irrelevant, prejudicial, and not in evidence, Carroll said. After court that afternoon, Father Quiñones
said he thought the judge showed a "degraded prejudice" toward
Latin Americans. Socorro Aguilar said she thought Carroll's strong
reaction to the Virgin's name was "a sign that he knows the power
of our Holy Mother."

Steve Cooper delivered his closing statement on the warm spring
morning of April 15. Corbett's lawyer displayed assurance, perhaps
with more reason than the other attorneys; the evidence against his
client was, at most, slight.

"Reno was forced to make wild leaps," Cooper said. "He had
to make an egregious, totally unsubstantiated foul shot." Cooper
quoted from Reno's closing: " 'Corbett was deeply involved. He was
well-known in Mexico for his illegal activities, not only there, but
here, in the way of bringing in aliens.'

"There's no support, not a shred, that the Mexican authorities
knew who Jim was. They watched him, taped him, investigated him
for three years, and this is what they would prove—that they saw
him three times in a church, once in his home, and once at a wedding. There was no evidence that anyone saw Corbett do anything
illegal. The way they conducted this investigation confirms what
Corbett said about them.

"Say there is a park," Cooper continued, "and the sign says, no
vehicles in the park. An ambulance goes into the park to save somebody's child who has fallen off the slide and cracked her head open.
The ambulance driver is charged with having a vehicle in the park.
First you decide, has it been proven beyond a reasonable doubt that
the ambulance was in the park? And second, you say, is this what is
meant by a vehicle? And then you apply the law, and you decide, is
this what is meant by the law?"

Cooper hurried on. He had suggested jury nullification, and
neither the judge nor Reno stopped him. This was the closest any of
the lawyers came to telling the jurors they could decide the case on
conscience.

"We, the American justice system, will be remembered and judged by what we do here," Cooper concluded. "If you put your seal of approval on this kind of case, with this kind of investigation, you will have done something the law does not allow—you will have convicted people on what has been far less than proof beyond a reasonable doubt. The only proof here is that the INS was annoyed, and that is not the stuff of which federal felonies are proven."

Cooper thanked the jury and sat down. He'd made it through his closing without Carroll interrupting him.

On the morning of the 17th, Judge Carroll read the jury their instructions. "You must follow the law as I give it to you whether you agree with it or not," he said. "You will recall that you took an oath promising to do so at the beginning of the case." Carroll gave each juror a copy of the instructions. Once in the jury room, their first piece of business was to pick Catherine Sheaffer as forewoman.

They deliberated nine days. During that time, they sent out only a few, insubstantial questions. They wanted a blackboard, which was allowed. They wanted to know if they could write on their jury instructions. Judge Carroll said no, because the papers were federal property. "He used every little trick he could to help the jury find us guilty," Hirsh said. "Giving each one their own set of instructions, and then telling them they can't write on them, as if the instructions were sacrosanct: 'This is my word, the word of the court.'"

MAY 1, 1986

The announcement that the jury had reached a verdict came just before 2 o'clock on a hot, early summer day. Reporters and sanctuary supporters waiting in the courthouse lined up for seats, and within minutes the gallery was full. It took another three-quarters of an hour to assemble all the defendants. The Corbetts were at home. Marianne Fife was at work, and when John called she drove over to Salpointe Catholic High School to pick up her youngest son, David. "This is good," she remembered telling him. Hirsh had assured her John would be acquitted.

In the courtroom, lawyers and defendants and their families accepted last-minute wishes of good luck. Marianne and David Fife moved to the front, and Hirsh saw them and gave Marianne a big grin. Ellen Yaroshefsky made the okay sign. The gallery was crowded with many long-time sanctuary supporters, among them County Supervisor David Yetman, Gary MacEoin, Father Elford, and Tim Nonn. Ken Kennon, who'd taken over Willis-Conger's job with the TEC task force, and other pastors from Tucson, Phoenix, and San Francisco were there. Gladys and Pat Corbett were up front, and Corbett's sister, a redhead from Prescott who was severely crippled by arthritis, had her wheelchair stationed in the aisle. Ann Russell and Joan Warfield, still members of the goat group, had lined up early and managed to get a seat. Chris Medvescek was there, along with the crush of national reporters who had reappeared after disappearing several days after the trial began. On the government side, Reno's wife and mother, both dressed in red and white, sat unsmiling. James Rayburn came in from a side door and took his place in front of the bar. A crowd of people who couldn't get seats gathered on the sidewalk in front of the courthouse.

The room quieted as Judge Carroll took the bench. He warned everyone that he would tolerate no outbursts or demonstrations while the verdict was being read. Then the jury filed in for the last time, and defendants and spectators searched their faces for a clue.

"Members of the jury, I am advised that you have arrived at a verdict. Is that correct?" Judge Carroll asked.

"That's correct," Catherine Sheaffer said. She handed the verdict forms to the bailiff, who carried them over to the judge. Carroll read through the verdicts quickly. "Very well," he said. "The clerk will please read the verdicts." A moment passed as the clerk gathered the papers. Carroll looked out over the courtroom, his lips pressed together.

The clerk began to read. "United States of America versus María del Socorro Pardo de Aguilar. We the jury in the above entitled and numbered case find the defendant María del Socorro Pardo de Aguilar guilty as charged to count one of the indictment."

A shock wave ran through the defendants and their families. Marianne Fife went numb. She knew if they convicted Socorro, many others, including her husband, would also be convicted. The clerk's clear, strong voice filled the room. With each guilty, the stunned defense lawyers and sanctuary supporters in the gallery sank a little lower in their seats. Reno and Miss Grabowski exchanged satisfied expressions, and then Reno turned to look at the specta-

tors. Marianne Fife began to cry. Hirsh slumped forward, his head
in his hands. Lynn Cobb, one of the jurors, began to cry. The defendants sat stone-faced as their fates were read. Socorro Aguilar,
Father Quiñones, Fife, Willis-Conger, Hutchison, and Sister Nicgorski were found guilty of conspiracy. All of these except Hutchison
had also been convicted of individual crimes; Aguilar and Father
Quiñones were guilty of one each, Fife and Willis-Conger of two
each, and Sister Nicgorski, the "travel agent" of the conspiracy, as
Reno had called her, was guilty of four. Wendy LeWin and Father
Clark were acquitted on the conspiracy count, but LeWin was found
guilty of one count of transporting, and Father Clark of one count of
harboring. The jury had returned convictions on 18 of the 30 counts
Reno ended up giving them to consider.

Three defendants were spared: Nena MacDonald, Mary K. Espinoza, and Jim Corbett. Espinoza couldn't help cracking a smile
of relief when she heard. At the moment Corbett learned he was
acquitted, Steve Cooper turned to look at him, to make sure, Corbett
said, he didn't do something self-destructive. Corbett later assured
his lawyer that he didn't mind being acquitted at all. "Survivor's
guilt isn't one of my hang-ups," he said.

Corbett was nevertheless very disappointed. "I was astounded
that they would convict," he said. "I couldn't understand how decent
people could do that sort of thing." It reminded him of a psycho-
logical test he'd read about in which two-thirds of the subjects gave
another person what they thought was a potentially lethal shock
when ordered to do so by someone posing as a scientist. They did
it even though the thought that they were hurting someone was
very upsetting to them. (Stanley Milgram, the psychologist who
conducted this experiment, also noted that outside observers vastly
overestimated his subjects' ability to defy the "scientist's" order. He
concluded it was difficult for people not in a hierarchical situation
to understand the pressure on those who were.) "And Judge Carroll
was a much stronger authority figure than anyone in those tests,"
Corbett said.

The clerk stopped reading. Judge Carroll polled the jury, asking
them each by name if this was their verdict. They said it was. The
judge thanked them for performing their duty as citizens and dismissed them. Carroll set sentencing for July 1, and when the defense
reminded him that the selective prosecution motion was still pend-

ing, Carroll said he'd hold a hearing on it in mid-June. At that time, he turned the motion down.

Defendants and their lawyers and families pushed through the ensuing confusion into the room where they had met throughout the trial. There, they collected themselves to face the press. Marianne Fife was crying. Hirsh was crying. Brosnahan was crying. Peggy Hutchison told the others, "We're going to walk out of here with our chins up, because we have done nothing wrong, and we have nothing to be ashamed of." Marianne Fife thought, "Peggy, whatever I feel is written all over my face."

Outside, with the afternoon sun slanting down Broadway, a procession of the convicted and their supporters surged into the street. Led by a cross held aloft, they walked toward San Augustine cathedral for a prayer service. Reno came out a side door and ducked into his black Porsche with *Star* reporter Daniel Browning. "I hope we're not going to get pelted," Reno said.

At his first press conference since the day of the indictment, the prosecutor couldn't help gloating just a bit. He said he was glad the jury had vindicated the government's position, and he also criticized the press for its biased coverage of the trial and the sanctuary movement in general. "You people in the media, what did you want us to do?" he asked. "Turn our heads?" His comment implied that the prosecution and trial were necessitated by media interest in sanctuary, just as the defense had maintained.

INS Commissioner Alan Nelson issued a statement to the Associated Press in Washington: "Above all, this case has demonstrated that no group, no matter how well-meaning or highly motivated, can arbitrarily violate the laws of the United States. The defendants, through this decision by a jury of their peers, must recognize that they have had their day in court and have been convicted through a fair and impartial system that presumes everyone is innocent until proven guilty."

Later in the afternoon, several hundred people filled a conference room at the Tucson Community Center to hear the defense lawyers' explanation of what happened. They had none. "I frankly don't understand it," said a glum-looking Hirsh. "We were happy with the way the evidence broke. I guess we just got the wrong jury." It turned out Catherine Sheaffer hadn't changed her party affiliation from Republican to Democrat, after all.

The second-guessing lasted long into the night. Steve Cooper commented to Corbett that, in his experience, had the defendants been bank robbers—any kind of real criminals—they would have been acquitted. "The judge's assumption of guilt was carried over to the jury," Cooper said. Corbett added, "The jury sees a political trial in terms of the government's perception of its being threatened, and it's hard to get them to take the burden of proof seriously."

The next morning, Catherine Sheaffer was quoted in the *Arizona Republic* saying that God had given her peace about the verdicts. "Render therefore unto Caesar the things that are Caesar's; and unto God the things that are God's," she said. "You see what the Lord says about government. You can protest your lot on this Earth, but in the end, you have to respect your government and its laws."

Other jurors weren't so sure they had done the right thing. "We followed the instructions to the letter, but I didn't walk out of there feeling good," one said. "I didn't want to do it, . . . but we had to," said another.

In an interview in the September 1986 issue of *American Lawyer* magazine, several jurors discussed their verdicts. Only two of them —Lynn Cobb, who worked in a bookstore, and Anna Browning, a Pima Community College student—were strongly for acquittal, and then only on the conspiracy count. Cobb had even suggested that perhaps the judge's instructions weren't the law, and perhaps they could be ignored. But Sheaffer quickly steered her away from that idea. "You have no right to be telling us that," Cobb quoted Sheaffer as saying.

With prodding by Sheaffer, the nurse, the computer programmer, and the "sanctuary is for the birds" man, the opposition fell away, until Browning was the last holdout. A day passed of everyone pressuring her, until finally she, too, collapsed, saying she feared what might happen to her if she hung the jury. (The others had told her the judge would keep them in there until they reached a verdict.) Browning refused to be interviewed by the lawyer's magazine; her mother said the trial experience had made her daughter sick.

Corbett called the jurors' attitude a "hireling mentality." So many people nowadays are told how to do their jobs, he said, that they become docile. Corbett contrasted this to the independence of early Americans, who developed self-reliance, he believed, from working their own land.

JULY 2, 1986

Jim Corbett's acquittal started his return to obscurity. In the summer of '86, he hastened the process by moving to an adobe house in Aravaipa Canyon, about 200 miles northeast of the city. Tall trees filled the canyon and a stream ran down the middle year-round, often rising to cut off the dirt road leading to the house. It was isolated enough for Corbett to have time to write, read, and go out by himself again, and for Pat to "decompress" from the past five years. The couple took their dogs and cats and mule, leaving the goats in town to be cared for by the Cabreros Andantes.

Corbett was glad the trial was over; he said he felt as if his brain had been atrophying for six months. He was also happy to be able to withdraw from the role of sanctuary spokesman. The movement could survive without him now, and although he still accepted speaking invitations from Quaker meetings, schools, or for debates with government officials, he preferred to devote himself to other projects. He held training sessions for sanctuary workers on new routes up from the border, and he was planning to put together a basic reference book on sanctuary services, modeled on the Central Committee for Conscientious Objectors' handbook. Corbett's main ambition now centered on his presanctuary concern for land redemption. He wanted to bring together a group of friends to buy a ranch. "We're developing a bill of rights for the land, to protect the community of plants and animals already there," Corbett said. "We want to work out a way for human beings to be part of a wildland community without destroying or seriously altering it."

The day of sentencing dawned muggy and gray in Tucson. A six-foot statue of Christ, made of plaster by an artist friend of Corbett's, hung from a lightpost across the street from the courthouse. People gathered in a light rain. Although her son was no longer part of the proceedings, Gladys Corbett joined Nena MacDonald and Mary K. Espinoza in wishing the convicted well. John Fife walked into court smiling, his arm around his wife. He looked content, but Marianne was still afraid Judge Carroll might have something special in store for her husband.

With Hirsh beside him, Fife gave his statement to the judge. He began by saying that as a pastor of a Christian church, he knew he had a spiritual and moral duty to save lives. What he learned from his involvement in sanctuary was that he had a legal duty as well. He continued:

From the Declaration of Independence to the trials at Nuremberg, our country has recognized that good citizenship requires that we disobey laws or officials whenever they mandate the violation of human rights. A government agency that commits crimes against humanity forfeits its claim to legitimacy.

We have heard a great deal this past year about authority—that the INS has the authority to decide who is an illegal alien, that the INS has the authority to decide who is deported, and that the courts have the authority to set aside international laws and treaties. I do not quarrel with those questions of authority, your honor. What I appeal to all of us to recognize is our responsibility first of all. The people of this blood-stained world have suffered throughout history from those who asserted authority without responsibility.

Mr. Reno in his closing argument said, "Reverend Fife cannot set up his own immigration service." That is a proper question. This society cannot withstand people taking the law into their own hands. That is why we have accepted the responsibility of being public, open, and truthful as we could be in all things. We only ask the INS to accept the same responsibility before this court. We must, all of us, even the INS, be willing to be judged by the people on all the evidence, on all the law, and on our best ideals and traditions as a nation.

It is also true that our nation and society cannot withstand violations of law and human rights by any agency or government. Justice Louis Brandeis said it most memorably: "If a government becomes a lawbreaker, it breeds contempt for the law; it invites every man to become a law unto himself." Your honor has remarked on more than one occasion during the trial that we had been publicly defiant, that our statements and actions had been defiant of the law and the INS. I apologize and beg forgiveness. I only intended to be public and responsible.

Sanctuary does not depend on any individual. It depends only on the truth, and the capacity of the human spirit to respond to suffering.

Judge Carroll thanked Fife and then asked the prosecutor if he had any comment before sentencing. Reno, who had remained mostly silent while Judge Carroll sentenced the others, could not stay silent now. He got to his feet.

"Your honor, the John Fife we have on tape is not the same John Fife we heard in this courtroom today," Reno said. "I would say there is serious question as to his motives and true interests. The word he used to agent Nixon—I'll never forget it."

There were a few gasps and groans in the audience. Was Reno pressing for a jail sentence for Fife?

"I'm trying to look at the positives," Judge Carroll said. "I'm not going to distinguish Mr. Fife from the others personally." Carroll gave Fife five years probation—the same sentence as the others. Marianne breathed a sigh of relief.

Father Quiñones spoke last. He said at no time had the Mexican authorities objected to what he was doing, and he was indignant that the INS had sent "spies" into his church and that Rayburn had gone to Hermosillo to make deals with professional coyotes—"true criminals in our country"—in order to catch sanctuary workers. "Both our countries have big problems," Father Quiñones said. "It is better for each to do his own dirty laundry at home."

That afternoon, as promised, Judge Carroll gave a short speech on his own perceptions of the trial. He began by saying he had received many letters about the sentencing, and they had been helpful to him in deciding what to do. One of the letters Carroll received was from Senator Dennis DeConcini, who addressed himself to John Fife's many contributions to the Tucson community and asked Carroll to "grant him the ability to continue his work." Another letter came from forty-seven members of the House of Representatives, including Morris Udall, Joe Moakley, Pat Schroeder, Claudine Schneider, and Henry B. Gonzalez. The members of Congress reminded Carroll that they had passed a Sense of Congress resolution recommending that Salvadorans be granted safe haven. A third letter Carroll received (it had been sent to Hirsh, and he passed it on to the judge) was from Amnesty International. It said AI would campaign for the sanctuary workers' release if Judge Carroll jailed them. (AI campaigned for "prisoners of conscience" as long as they had not used or advocated the use of violence.) Carroll didn't say if these three letters had had any effect on his decision to sentence the sanctuary workers to probation. But, as in his sentencing to house arrest of the four who refused to testify, Carroll appeared conscious of the public perception of his actions.

The judge did say that he felt the sanctuary workers were sincere in their motivation. "However," he continued, "the system works. It works slowly, but that's not the fault of the system. It's the fault of the people who use it." Carroll cited the Orantes-Hernández case as one in which the system had been made to work, and he said perhaps one of the reasons why Salvadoran and Guatemalan asylum cases were being turned down was because "the attorneys are not of the caliber of those here." The defense lawyers looked at each other in disbelief.

"These procedures take time and hard work, and don't have the allure of a trial such as this, the media attention, the applause, the television appearances. It's easy to say the system doesn't work, and we're not going to use it and we have been disappointed by it. If there are bad procedures in Nogales, or no procedures, then action should be taken—not in this proceeding, not by violating the law—but by making fuller and more determined use of the system."

Judge Carroll's comments were a disappointment to the defendants and their lawyers. "He believes that the law always will result in justice, and the problem was that we were just not skillful or bright enough to use the law like it should have been used," Fife said.

Why, if Carroll believed that the defendants' violation of the law was deliberate, did he not sentence them to jail? Attorney Tom Chandler, Carroll's friend, said *he* would have sentenced them to jail, because presumably that's what the sanctuary workers wanted —to suffer for their beliefs and call further attention to their unjust convictions. "Deliberate violation of the law is meaningless if you don't pay the price," Chandler said. Judge Vela in Texas employed similar logic when, in response to Jack Elder's comment that "I would like somehow to open people's eyes and compare the illegality of [my] action with the daily slaughter that goes on in El Salvador," Vela said, "You know, I thought a lot about that. I could have nurtured the approach that is being taken. I could have given you 30 years and I could have given her [Stacey Merkt] 20. But you two don't deserve that."

Judge Carroll apparently didn't think the defendants deserved that either. "This trial was about vindicating the government and branding what these people did as illegal," Hirsh said. Once that was accomplished, Carroll could show that he was fair and merciful, after all.

If Reno was disappointed by the sentences, he didn't show it. He commented to reporters that first-time felons convicted of nonviolent crimes are usually given probation. "The convictions were the most startling deterrent they're ever going to receive in a court of law," he said. He added that he expected the convictions would make people think twice in the future before joining the sanctuary movement.

But the trial only seemed to result in a standoff between the government and the sanctuary workers. The movement had continued to grow during the trial, with more churches and religious orders, the city of Los Angeles, and the state of New Mexico declaring themselves sanctuaries. (New Mexico's declaration was rescinded when a Republican governor took office in 1987.) The TEC task force and Trsg found new converts, despite the loss of several defendants to other pursuits. Dave Sholin took charge of a suit that Southside and several other churches had pending against the government for using concealed recording devices on church property. That suit was dismissed in October, but as Sholin's reinvolvement demonstrated, government prosecution had led more, not fewer, people to work for sanctuary. For their part, the convicted were personally relieved at the sentences. At the same time, they could not help comparing what Americans suffered for their beliefs—probation, or the experience of the "Naco Five"—to what happened to Guatemalans and Salvadorans who disagreed with their government.

Jim Corbett felt the biggest lesson of the trial was that more education needed to be done. "It's in the nature of politicians and governments to want to get rid of all restraints on their exercise of power," he said. "That's something the people who founded this country were so concerned with—how do you get control of these folks once you've given them positions of power? Checks and balances can correct some of this, keeping their various powers separate, but you also have to have a community that is the ultimate check on government absolutism. The community has to take the responsibility of saying no. 'We have basic liberties you're not going to infringe on, we have human rights you're not going to violate, and we're going to exercise them regardless of your use of coercive powers that you have.' That's the only way you can keep the governed governing their government—by exercising your rights and liberties and defending those of others. It's built into our kind of system, and it's something that needs to be learned by a lot of people, including potential jurors.

"It's very important to disobey the Judge Carrolls of this world," Corbett continued, "the people who have such contempt for human rights, and simply look at the letter of the law, and don't even do that, when it goes against their defense of the authorities who hold office. You have to hold them accountable, not only by defending the law, but by extending the rule of law among nations. The only way for that to happen is for communities within various societies to do it. We're not going to get a law among nations either by trying to form a super-state where sovereignty is given to it, or by the nations suddenly giving up power voluntarily. You've got to hold them accountable and have the social structure that does it, and then the legal realities will follow."

With his ranch, Corbett hoped to develop such a community. He envisioned it as a group of friends who would live sanctuary among themselves. "I am interested in the whole development of a land ethic in which there is protective, symbiotic community at work," he said. "Human beings have an enormous responsibility to bring into full, reflective consciousness the community that exists among all living things. Life is in fact among us, rather than in us. Sanctuary, in its broadest sense, extends far beyond Central America and specific human refugees to the need for harmonious community among all that lives."

WAY WILL OPEN

On August 7, 1987, fifteen months after the Tucson sanctuary convictions, the presidents of five Central American nations gathered
in Guatemala City to sign an historic peace treaty. The agreement,
developed from the Contadora plan by Costa Rican President Oscar
Arias, called for a cease-fire, negotiation with rebel groups, and res-
toration of civil rights in countries that had suspended them. The
signing was a bold first step toward Central American regional self-
determination. It was also an expression of the popular sentiment
that, in the words of Guatemalan President Vinicio Cerezo, "Central
America is tired of suffering and dying."

Tragically, implementation of this plan remained a distant dream.
The U.S. government had interests to protect and would probably
not allow Central America to go off and make its own peace. The
military leaders of every country in the region except Costa Rica
were unlikely to abandon violence and coercion as their means of
keeping people in line. (The Arias plan did not call for a halt to foreign military aid to governments.) The rebels in El Salvador, Guatemala, and Nicaragua would also resist laying down their arms to
the same people they had just been trying to overthrow. Central
American civilians were still pawns to the powers on both sides who
would stop at nothing short of total victory.

Corbett remembered when he learned first-hand that the left cared
as little about human lives as the right. In 1983, through the Nogales
grapevine, he and Father Quiñones discovered that several members
of a Mexican left-wing party were planning to turn them over to the
immigration authorities for helping refugees. The leftists apparently

thought refugees should be forced to stay and fight instead of running away. This group was also planning to turn in any Salvadorans they found working in northern Mexico, until Corbett met with them and convinced them to abandon their plans. As long as both sides continued to violate refugee rights, Corbett believed, sanctuary in some form would be necessary.

There was no shortage of refugees arriving at the Arizona border in the year following the trial. The Tucson sanctuary groups conducted crossings on the average of once every other week, and Corbett now routinely informed the INS that undocumented people were coming in from the border to apply for asylum. The Tucson INS office accepted these asylum requests without arresting the applicants. Four sanctuary workers, including Ken Kennon and Rabbi Joseph Weizenbaum, were picked up with refugees near the border in July 1987, but the Border Patrol let them go without even bothering to take fingerprints. As long as sanctuary operated without a lot of publicity, the government seemed content to look the other way and pretend it was, as Don Reno said, "virtually dead."

The movement, rather than dying out, continued to grow. By the spring of 1987, some four hundred churches in the United States had declared sanctuary. John Fife went to Houston at the end of 1986 to receive the Rothko-Chapel Human Rights Award on behalf of the movement, and in September 1986, John Fife, Peggy Hutchison, and A. Bates Butler, III, went to Holland to meet with twenty-seven representatives of European churches who were interested in expanding the sanctuary concept to their countries. (In May, four hundred church delegates from forty-two countries meeting in France had passed a resolution supporting the convicted.) The European church workers were concerned about their governments' recent deportations of Chileans, Turkish Kurds, Sri Lankans, and Zairians who had come to Europe seeking political asylum. They felt these policies increased racist attitudes and scapegoating of refugees for Europe's social and economic problems, not to mention the hardship created for refugees.

Aside from these efforts, the primary focus of sanctuary in Tucson was now outreach to Mexico and Central America. The TEC collected and sent a planeload of food, clothing, blankets, and medical supplies to San Salvador after the city was hit by a major earthquake in October 1986. (Judge Carroll refused to let Fife and Hutchison accompany the plane to El Salvador at Christmas.) At the same time, Southside, St. Mark's, and several other churches had set up a program in which groups took turns going to El Salvador for one to three weeks. Two young members of Southside's congregation, Tim Walrath and David Holliday, went to the Batania refugee camp as part of Project Amistad in January 1987. Dorothy Anderson, an attender of Pima Friends Meeting, reported in the meeting newsletter on a talk given by Walrath and Holliday at the Northwest Community Friends Church in February:

The picture they gave us of life in the camp was one of uprooted people whose homes and lands had been bombed, who longed to be back home, yet who still were warm and caring toward others. Fresh vegetables and fruits were scarce, but after the earthquake, the refugees in this camp gave half their fresh food to earthquake victims.

Project Amistad was started to "build a mutual friendship of support and concern with the people of Batania." A North American presence in the camp has had a restraining effect on the El Salvadoran soldiers who used to come to harass and capture people. While David Holliday was there, he was summoned from the 9-foot-deep latrine he was digging to "come because the soldiers are here." The soldiers, with fingers on their triggers, were saying they had come to help. A quick-witted Canadian nurse said, "No, thanks. Your uniforms would scare the little children," and the soldiers left.

David and Tim met with human rights workers and with people who had been recently detained by the government. Many people are detained without charge for 15 days "on suspicion," which is legal in El Salvador. During this time they are tortured by near suffocation in plastic bags, a method which leaves no physical scars. Under such torture they are forced to sign blank sheets of paper. Later their "confessions" are typed in. A typical "confession" would be, "I said I was collecting money for the church to help the poor but actually I was giving it to the Communist guerrillas." The "confessions" are then publicized to undermine people's faith in the church and its workers. Tim and David felt blessed to have been with people who carry on with faith and courage despite such intimidation and deception.

These two young men pointed out that money sent by the U.S. government to the Salvadoran government never helps the people. Even U.S. government earthquake relief went from the Salvadoran government into the banks and from there to property owners. Poor people, who were the hardest hit, got none of it.

After some days the two young men were questioning their usefulness—they weren't as good at latrine digging as they'd expected, and they couldn't carry as much water as most of the women. One of the women said, "Don't worry. As long as you sleep here we won't get killed." So they brought back the message, "If you feel your life is meaningless, just go to El Salvador and sleep and you will be a hero!"

Walrath and Holliday's report provided grim contradiction to the U.S. government's characterization of El Salvador as a "fledgling democracy." Persecution of Salvadoran church workers remained everyday occurrences, and twenty-one American church workers who came with earthquake relief in mid-June were expelled. In July, the country's unflinching rule by military terrorism took on an international dimension, when for the first time Salvadoran death squads reportedly attacked people in the United States. The death squads targeted Central American members of the Los Angeles chapter of CISPES (the Committee in Solidarity with the People of El Salvador). A 24-year-old Salvadoran woman said she was forced at knifepoint into a van, blindfolded, and then interrogated about her friends and political activities by two men who spoke Spanish with Salvadoran accents. She was beaten, burned with cigarettes, cut on the tongue and hands, and raped repeatedly with a stick as they drove around the city. Ten days later, another Guatemalan refugee was also abducted and questioned in Los Angeles. She was released unharmed in Pomona, about 40 miles east of the city. A third Salvadoran who'd been granted asylum in the United States, Marta Alicia Rivera, received a death threat at her home in Los Angeles that contained almost the same phrase as two notes she'd received in El Salvador before her kidnapping and torture there six years earlier. "Flowers in the desert die," it read. Eighteen other CISPES members also received death threats.

The FBI initially declined to investigate these events, citing lack of jurisdiction. Harold Ezell, Western Regional Commissioner for the INS, stated he thought the incidents were staged as part of the sanctuary movement's public-relations campaign. After protests by Massachusetts Representative Joe Moakley and California Representative Don Edwards, the FBI agreed to launch an investigation.

Whether bowing to public and congressional pressure or not, government officials were grudgingly beginning to acknowledge the claims of Central American refugees. About half the Salvadoran and Guatemalan asylum applications that came before the immigration court in Arizona between October 1985 and July 1987 were

approved. (The nationwide approval rate, however, remained below
3 percent.) The INS now released many Central Americans on their
own recognizance, apparently because of overcrowding in the detention centers. The most startling change in government policy was the
State Department's reversal on the DeConcini-Moakley bill. Officials feared that a mass exodus of Salvadorans now living in the
United States (prompted by the new immigration bill that made it
illegal to hire undocumented workers) would spell disaster for El
Salvador, straining the overburdened economy to the breaking point
and perhaps providing fresh recruits for the guerrillas. Claiming it
was for economic, not political, reasons, the State Department announced it would support the bill (which now also included Nicaraguans). The Justice Department still opposed DeConcini-Moakley,
saying under no circumstances should safe haven be granted to
"economic migrants." Supporters expected a close vote.

The U.S. government appeared to be adopting the approach of
the Mexican government toward refugees and church workers: Tacit
acceptance, but always with the threat of punishment for breaking
the law. At the beginning of 1987, Stacey Merkt, who was preg-
nant with her first child, went to jail to serve the almost six-month
sentence Judge Vela had given her on her second conviction. (Two
months later, Merkt was released and placed under house arrest for
the duration of her sentence.) In March, the Supreme Court refused
to hear Merkt's and Jack Elder's appeal that their activities were
protected under the First Amendment guarantee of freedom of religion. The appeal of the Tucson sanctuary workers' convictions to
the Ninth Circuit was pending. "Justice is a process, not a result,"
attorney Tom Chandler said. The convicted, while aware that the
wheels of justice turned slowly, expected eventually to be vindicated
in court.

Jim and Pat Corbett moved back into town in the spring of 1987.
They lived in a trailer on the south side of Tucson, near the San
Xavier del Bac mission, and Corbett got back into refugee work. He
continued to champion the cause of nonviolence in his writings, and
he also continued to share his work primarily with other Quakers.
Corbett recognized much education needed to be done within his
own faith. Some Quakers were confused about the use of revolu-
tionary counterviolence, believing, as most of the world does, that
violence is sometimes a necessary evil. Corbett presented the oppo-

site view: nonviolence as the answer, the first step to solving our problems, not the last. His experience with thousands of victims of civil war over the past six years had only confirmed his belief that violence solved nothing. St. Paul said, "If you want peace, seek justice." Corbett turned that around to say, "If you want justice, seek peace."

Pacifism is often characterized as a copout, as fuzzy-headed utopianism, as pathetically naive. Yet Corbett had demonstrated by his work with refugees that nonviolence can be at least as powerful and effective a weapon as violence. His positive vision of the future kept him from being cynical or defeatist, even though his views were in a tiny minority, he was misunderstood and disliked by many of his sanctuary co-workers, and he had no plans or aspirations to lead a mass movement. He was able to do this because his philosophy was based on faith. He had faith that the Central American peace process could work, if given a chance. He had faith that the peaceful actions of individuals, or small groups, could make as much of a difference as the cries of thousands. He was right.

NOTES

The Inner Light

Page 2, paragraph 1: Woolman's quote appeared on page 7 of *The Journal and Major Essays of John Woolman*, edited by Phillips P. Moulton (Oxford University Press, New York, 1971).

Page 2, paragraph 4: George Macauley Trevelyan was quoted on page 200 of Thomas E. Drake's *Quakers and Slavery in America* (Yale University Press, New Haven, 1950), an excellent historical study of the subject.

A Quiet Testimony

Scenes in this section are depicted in dramatic re-creation, which means the author relied on the primary and secondary sources listed below for descriptions of events which she did not personally witness. In certain cases, statements of minor characters rendered as hearsay to the author were written as quotes. This was done for the purpose of moving the story along, and the author apologizes to those offended by this technique. The credibility of the sources of these quotes is for readers to judge. All locations, unless noted, were visited by the author.

1. Pages 6–12: The major source on the tragedy in Organ Pipe National Monument was Aron Spilken's book *Escape!* (New American Library, New York, 1983). Spilken conducted extensive interviews with survivors, who quoted statements attributed to Carlos Rivera and the Doll-boss. The names Berta, Guadalupe, and Don Cruz were pseudonyms used by Spilken. Other sources on the victims' true names (Carlos Rivera and Claudia Huezo) and identities were "Smuggler killed 4 women, claim desert survivors,"

by Randy Collier, *Arizona Republic*, July 11, 1980, and "Fearful refugees refuse interviews," by Keith Rosenblum, *Arizona Daily Star*, July 11, 1980.

Pages 7–8: History of ORDEN and Archbishop Rivera y Damas's estimate were on pages 77 and 181 of *Salvador Witness* (Simon and Schuster, New York, 1984). Ana Carrigan's book tells the story of Jean Donovan, one of four American church women killed in El Salvador in December 1980. The fate of the young man who failed to show up for his second stint in the Salvadoran National Guard was recounted on page 44 of *Escape!*. Statement of the vicar of Chalatenango was in a June 1980 letter from Jean Donovan to Father Michael Crowley, quoted on page 177 of *Salvador Witness*.

2. Pages 12–19: Details of the conversation on the night of May 4, 1981, were obtained from the author's personal interviews with Jim and Pat Corbett, Frank Shutts, and Jim Dudley, in July and August 1985 in Tucson, Hermosillo, and Albuquerque. Other major sources were transcripts of interviews with Jim and Pat Corbett and Jim Dudley provided to the author by John Longenecker, a Los Angeles-based movie producer who researched many of the events portrayed in the first half of this book for a proposed film on Corbett. Longenecker conducted his interviews in June and July of 1984 in Tucson and by telephone to Albuquerque.

Page 13: See "The Goat Cheese Economy of the South Baja Sierras," by J.A. Corbett, *Dairy Goat Journal*, July 1979.

Pages 14–15: Quotes are Jim Dudley's recollection to author of what was said at the time.

Page 15, paragraph 7: Corbett's teachers were quoted in "On the line," by Linda Witt, *Chicago Tribune* Sunday magazine, May 5, 1985. Gladys Corbett's statement was made to author, fall 1986, Tucson.

Pages 16–18: *Salvador Witness*; *Liberation Theology* by Phillip Berryman (Pantheon, New York, 1987); and *Sanctuary: The New Underground Railroad*, by Renny Golden and Michael McConnell (Orbis Books, Maryknoll, N.Y., 1986) were sources on Salvadoran history and the Santa Fe Group Paper. Archbishop Romero was quoted on page 157 of *Salvador Witness*.

Page 18: Information on Zoila Serpas, Santana Chirino Amaya, and the quote from Blaise Bonpane were published on pages 42 and 44 of *No Promised Land: American Refugee Policies and the Rule of Law*, by Gary MacEoin and Nivita Riley (Oxfam America, Boston, MA, 1982).

3. Pages 19–22: Major sources for the events of May 5, 1981, were the author's interviews with Jim Corbett and Father Elford, conducted in Tucson in August 1985, and John Longenecker's interviews with Corbett and Elford in Tucson, June 1984.

Page 19, paragraph 3; page 20, paragraph 1: Corbett's quotes of himself were made in an interview with KNST reporter Paul Weich, Tucson, September 6, 1984. Weich provided a tape of the interview to the author.

Page 21: Enrique Molina Parada is a pseudonym. Corbett quoted Molina's mother's letter in an interview with John Longenecker, June 1984.

Pages 21–22: Border patrolman and prison guard were quoted by Corbett in his first "Dear Friends" letter (May 12, 1981), published in *Borders and Crossings*, by James A. Corbett, Tucson, 1986. Corbett also provided the description of the Santa Cruz County Jail, which was not visited by the author.

4. Pages 22–24: Ana Daisie's story was related to the author by Jim and Pat Corbett during the fall of 1985. Corbett also told her story to John Longenecker in June 1984. The name Ana Daisie is a pseudonym. Quotes by Ana Daisie and Margo Cowan were attributed by Corbett.

5. Pages 24–28: Information for this chapter was obtained from the author's personal interviews with Father Elford, John and Marianne Fife, Jim and Pat Corbett, Dave Sholin, Gary MacEoin, Lupe Castillo, and Mike Smith, in Tucson, June and July of 1986, and with Tim Nonn in August 1985. Father Elford provided a copy of the prayer sheet used at the May 21, 1981, vigil.

Page 25, paragraph 2: Fife's quote was in an interview with him in the March 1985, *Sojourners*, conducted by Jim Wallis and Joyce Hollyday, in Tucson.

Page 26, paragraph 3: Marianne Fife quoted by her husband, in interview with author, Tucson, February 1987.

Page 27, paragraph 4: *This Ground Is Holy*, by Ignatius Bau (Paulist Press, New York, 1985), cited the end of World War II as the beginning of official U.S. recognition of refugees and of organized church efforts to resettle them. The Christmas 1984 issue of *Shalom*, newsletter of St. Mark's Presbyterian Church, provided information on the Tucson Ecumenical Council.

6. Pages 28–31: Sources on the May 30, 1981, visit to El Centro were the author's interview with Corbett (Tucson, May 1986), John Longenecker's interview with Corbett (Tucson, June 1984), and an affadavit on the incident Corbett filed with Los Angeles-based immigration attorney Bruce Bowman on May 30, 1981.

Pages 28–29: Rubén's quote and information about his background were contained in a transcript of a November 15, 1981, interview with him in Tucson, conducted by Paul Mirocha and translated by Ian Dodd for the Tucson Ecumenical Council. The number killed at Archbishop Romero's funeral was recorded by Jean Donovan in her diary (*Salvador Witness*, page 160).

Page 29: Description of El Centro, not visited by the author, was provided by Corbett and page 49 of *No Promised Land*. "Detention center ends roads, shatters dreams," the last of a five-part series, *Escape from El Salvador*, by Dale Maharidge, published August 26–30, 1984, in the *Sacramento Bee*, provided numbers and percentages of Salvadorans in El Centro.

Page 30: Quotes by Enrique Molina and J.E. Aguirre were attributed by Corbett.

7. Pages 31–35: Sources on the events of June 4, 1981, were the author's interviews with Jim and Pat Corbett, Ann Russell, and Joan Warfield, in Tucson, July 1986, Russell's diary entry for the morning of June 5, 1981, and John Longenecker's interviews with Corbett, Russell, and Warfield in Tucson, June 1984.

Pages 31–32: See *Introductory Goatwalking*, by Jim Corbett, Tucson, 1978.

Pages 44–47: The location of the hidden store is disguised. Doña María is a pseudonym. Quotes by anonymous residents of Panama 24, Doña María, and Chico were attributed and translated by Corbett, Russell, and Warfield.

8. Pages 35–39: Major sources for the scene at Sacred Heart Church on June 5, 1981, were John Longenecker's interviews with Jim Corbett and Father Elford (Tucson, June 1984) and Jim Corbett's "Dear Friends" letter of July 6, 1981. Additional sources were the author's interviews with Corbett and Elford en route from Tucson to Nogales, August 1985, and with Father Elford, Tucson, June 1986.

Pages 35–36: Quotes by Gladys Corbett were in "On the line," by Linda Witt, *Chicago Tribune* Sunday magazine, May 5, 1985.

Page 36: Sources on Quakerism were an article by Doug Tipple in the newsletter of the Pima Monthly Meeting, January 1986, and *On Doing Good*, by Gerald Jonas (Scribners, New York, 1971).

Pages 37–38: Corbett's words and poem were published on pages 8, 10, and 11 of *Borders and Crossings*.

Pages 38–39: Quotes by Father Noriega, Father Quiñones, Elford, and Corbett were attributed by Corbett and Elford during an interview with John Longenecker, Tucson, June 1984. Father Quiñones's remarks were translated by Corbett and Elford.

9. Pages 39–43: Sources on the prison visit were the author's interviews with Corbett and Father Elford (Tucson, May and June 1986), and with Father Quiñones (Nogales, July 1986).

Page 40, paragraph 5: "Viva Padre Quiñones" observed by author during July 1986 visit to the prison.

Page 41, paragraph 1: Father Quiñones quoted himself in July 1986 interview with author. The interview was conducted in Spanish and translated by the author.

Page 42, paragraph 1: Information on Mexican treatment of Central American refugees was obtained from Father Quiñones (in Nogales, July 1986), and in a phone conversation with Ricardo Chavira from his office at Time, Inc., in Washington, D.C., on February 17, 1987 (at which time Chavira made his quoted remark). Additional information was provided by telephone and mail from José Luis Pérez Canchola, of the Centro De Información Y Estudios Migratorios in Tijuana, Mexico, and by Nativo Lopez, formerly with the American Friends Service Committee, in a telephone interview from Santa Ana, California, February 1987. Gary MacEoin reported in *No Promised Land* that the U.S. government was paying a "head fee" for each Salvadoran detained in northern Mexico, but the author was unable to confirm that this was the case.

10. Pages 43–48: Sources for the incident at the INS office were the author's interviews with Corbett (Tucson, May and July 1986) and with Bill Johnston (Tucson, June 1986). An additional source was John Longenecker's June 1984 interview with Corbett.

Page 44: *No Promised Land* provided information on asylum rates and the United Nations' study.

Pages 44–45: "No Refugees Need Apply," by Claudia Dreifus, in the February 1987 *Atlantic*, was the source for the internal INS study, Maurice Inman's reaction to it, the GAO report, and Senator Arlen Specter's quote.

Page 45: The Supreme Court decision was reported in the March 10, 1987, *Arizona Daily Star* ("Justices ease rules on asylum") by AP reporter James H. Rubin.

Page 46: INS employee's quote attributed by Corbett in interview with author, Tucson, July 1986.

Page 47, paragraph 5: Information on Extended Voluntary Departure was provided by Corbett and by a March 5, 1985, statement by Church World Service.

Page 48: Johnston's statements made in interview with author, Tucson, June 1986.

11. Pages 48–51: The author's interviews with Jim and Pat Corbett, John and Marianne Fife, Father Elford, Gary MacEoin, Dave Sholin, Mike Smith, Ken Kennon, and Lupe Castillo in Tucson in June 1986 were major sources on the meeting at Picture Rocks. Additional sources were John Longenecker's 1984 interviews with Fife, Corbett, and Elford.

Page 49: Descriptions of conditions at El Centro were provided by *No Promised Land* and by Ken Kennon, in a June 1986 interview with the author in Tucson. *No Promised Land* was also the source on the Orantes-Hernández case.

Page 50: Sources on the bond-out were Corbett, Ken Kennon, and Father Richard Sinner (interviewed by the author in Tucson in February 1986) and John Longenecker's interview with Father Elford in June 1984.

Page 51, paragraph 2: Corbett's August 13, 1985, letter to Assistant INS Commissioner Delia B. Combs was on page 176 of *Borders and Crossings*. Testimony of two deportees who saw a third taken away when the plane landed in San Salvador was reported on page 44 of *No Promised Land*.

12. Pages 51–57: Most of the information in this chapter was obtained from the author's interviews with Jim and Pat Corbett in Tucson, August 1985 and June 1986. Unless noted, all quotes by Corbett in this chapter were made during those interviews. "On the line," by Linda Witt, in the May 5, 1985, *Chicago Tribune* Sunday magazine, was also a source on details of Corbett's past.

Page 52: Gladys Corbett was quoted in the May 5, 1985, *Chicago Tribune* Sunday magazine. Jim Corbett was quoted in the August 25, 1985, *Boston Globe* ("Sanctuary drive said to be growing," by Jean Caldwell).

Page 54: Pat Corbett was quoted in the *Chicago Tribune* Sunday magazine, May 5, 1985.

Page 56: Corbett's clipping was from "Planes don't change guerrilla war," by Jack Foisie of the *Los Angeles Times* News Service, as reported in the March 4, 1965, *Arizona Republic*.

13. Pages 57–61: The author's interviews with John and Marianne Fife (Tucson, June and July 1986) were the major source for this chapter. Additional sources were the author's June 1986 interview with Pat Corbett and John Longenecker's June 1984 interviews with Corbett and Fife.

Page 57, paragraph 4: John Fife to author, Tucson, June 1986.

Page 58: Marianne Fife to author, Tucson, July 1986.

Page 59: Corbett and Fife quoted themselves in the June 1984 interview with Longenecker. Pat Corbett's statement was made to author, fall 1985.

Page 60: Corbett's statement to the National Council of the Churches of Christ consultation on immigration, in Washington, D.C., on January 28–30, 1982, was on page 28 of *Borders and Crossings*.

Page 60, paragraph 5: Millie Paylock in a telephone interview with author, Tucson, February 1987.

14. Pages 61–65: The major source on Corbett's trip to southern Mexico was selections from his diary and letter to Pat that appeared on pages 17–22

of *Borders and Crossings*. An additional source was the author's interview with Corbett in Klondyke, Arizona, August 1986. All descriptions of scenes, quotes of other characters, and translations were provided by Corbett. The author did not visit southern Mexico or Guatemala.

15. Pages 65–68: Major sources for this chapter were the author's interviews with Corbett, Fife, Gary MacEoin, Lupe Castillo, Mike Smith, Tim Nonn, Dave Sholin, Father Elford, and Ken Kennon in Tucson in June and July 1986. Other sources were John Longenecker's interviews with Corbett, Fife, and Elford in June 1984.

Page 65: Fife's paraphrase of the INS message was made to John Longenecker, Tucson, June 1984.

Page 66: Mark Van Der Hout was quoted on page 41 of *No Promised Land*.

Page 66, paragraph 3: Source on "Sense of Congress" resolution was an August 4, 1987, letter to the author from Jim McGovern, legislative aide to Massachusetts Representative John Joseph Moakley.

Page 66, paragraphs 4–5: Fife to John Longenecker, Tucson, June 1984.

Page 67: A copy of Wagner's October 22, 1981, letter was printed on page 35 of *Borders and Crossings*.

Page 68: Sources on churches that joined the sanctuary declaration were page 23 of *Sanctuary: A Resource Guide for Understanding and Participating in the Central American Refugees' Struggle*, edited by Gary MacEoin (Harper & Row, New York, 1985), and page 48 of *Sanctuary: The New Underground Railroad*, by Golden and McConnell. An additional source was the letter sent by Tim Nonn on behalf of the Tucson Ecumenical Council Task Force on Central America to churches considering joining the sanctuary action, dated March 11, 1982.

16. Pages 68–73: The primary source for this chapter was a TEC task force videotape of the March 24, 1982, sanctuary declaration and ecumenical service, viewed by the author in August 1986. Additional sources were "Tucson a hub of Salvadoran 'railroad,'" by Randy Udall and James W. Wyckoff, *Tucson Citizen*, March 17, 1982; "Tucson church will harbor Salvadorans," by Mark Turner, *Arizona Daily Star*, March 25, 1982; and "Agent urged caution in taking on 'Frito Bandito' railroad," by Carol Ann Bassett and Sandy Tolan, *Arizona Republic*, June 30, 1985. The author's interviews with John Fife and Jim Corbett during February 1987 in Tucson, and with Randy Udall, by telephone from Carbondale, Colorado, in June 1987, provided additional information. A copy of INS agent James Rayburn's June 30, 1983, memo on the "El Salvadorian Underground Railroad" was filed with federal district court in Tucson in November 1985.

Page 69: Alfredo is a pseudonym.

Into the Breach

Page 75, paragraph 1: "Letters came from mainstream, even conservative congregations." See "Illegal Alien Smuggling: New Partner," by Larry Stammer, in the February 7, 1983, *Los Angeles Times*.

Page 76: Pages 48–49 of *Sanctuary: The New Underground Railroad*, by Golden and McConnell, and the January 1985 issue of *Basta!*. Larry Stammer's February 7, 1983, *Los Angeles Times* article was the source on the number of sanctuary churches in March 1983. Weakland's and Hunthausen's support was cited on pages 26–27 of *Sanctuary*, edited by Gary MacEoin.

Pages 76–77: Sources on Central America were "Archbishop condemns air strikes," an Associated Press story as reported in the January 13, 1986, *Arizona Daily Star*; *Sanctuary: The New Underground Railroad*, pages 120–21; and "Understanding El Salvador," a booklet published by the American Friends Service Committee.

Page 77, paragraph 2: Peter Larrabee was quoted on page 57 of *No Promised Land*. The monthly average of Guatemalans and Salvadorans deported in 1983 was provided by the INS statistics office, in a August 4, 1987, telephone interview with the author from Washington, D.C. Departure data are reported by airlines, steamship companies, and port authorities, and do not include aliens required to depart directly under government safeguard or those immediately turned out of the United States.

Information on DeConcini-Moakley bill was provided to author by mail from Jim McGovern, aide to Representative Joe Moakley, August 1987.

Pages 77–78: Corbett's statement to author, Tucson, fall 1985. Corbett's October 28, 1982, speech in Austin was reprinted on page 39 of *Borders and Crossings*.

Page 78, paragraph 2: Fife's statement was made to John Longenecker, Tucson, June 1984. Leon Ring was quoted in " 'Underground railroad' still runs in the open," by Beverly Mcdlyn, *Arizona Daily Star*, December 25, 1982.

Page 78, paragraph 3: Joyce quoted in "U.S. churches defy law—form network to harbor Salvadoran refugees," by Christina Ravashiere, *Christian Science Monitor*, August 20, 1982.

Page 79: Anonymous INS official quoted in "The Border Breaker," by Carla Hall, *Washington Post*, July 23, 1983.

Page 81: Don Dale was quoted in "Illegal Alien Smuggling: New Partner," in the February 7, 1983, *Los Angeles Times*.

Information on the Chicago Religious Task Force's position was from a December 3, 1983, CRTFCA letter to Jim Corbett, Phil Conger, and John Fife, and the author's telephone interview with Renny Golden, from Chicago, August 1985.

Pages 81–82: TEC and Trsg guidelines from "Discussion Guide for Tucson Sanctuary Volunteers, October-November 1984," *Borders and Crossings*, pages 122–23.

Page 82, paragraph 2: Corbett to author, Tucson, February 1987. The September 25, 1984, statement of the TEC Task Force was in the January 1985 *Basta!*.

Page 82, paragraph 3: Corbett to author, Tucson, February 1987.

Page 83: "Some Consideration On Direction For The Sanctuary Movement," and "Statement of Faith of the CRTFCA," *Basta!*, January 1985.

Page 83, paragraph 2: *Borders and Crossings*, pages 115 and 120.

Page 84: Renny Golden, in telephone interview with author, August 1985. On numbers of sanctuary sites, see Bau, *This Ground Is Holy*, page 12.

Page 85: Chicago Task Force estimate in "Crackdown on Sanctuary," by Lindie Bosniak and Jane Rasmussen, *Report on the Americas*, May/June 1984.

Pages 85–87: Portions of Corbett's March 21, 1985, debate with Laura Dietrich in Santa Fe were on pages 143–146 of *Borders and Crossings*. The ACLU survey was also discussed on page 69 of *Sanctuary: The New Underground Railroad*, and in Claudia Dreifus's February 1987 *Atlantic* article.

Pages 87–88: Bau, *This Ground Is Holy*, pages 76–79.

Page 88, paragraph 2: *Borders and Crossings*, page 93.

Page 88, paragraph 3: Corbett's and Fife's comments on Cruz and Graham were made in interviews with author, Tucson, June 1986. Corbett mentioned the government study in "Indictments target sanctuary members," by Mark Turner, Ernie Heltsley, and James H. Maish, *Arizona Daily Star*, January 15, 1985.

Page 89, paragraph 2: Bau, pages 80 and 82.

Page 89, paragraph 3: *Sanctuary*, edited by MacEoin, and *Sanctuary: The New Underground Railroad* were sources on the names and numbers of sanctuary supporters at the end of 1984.

Page 89, paragraph 4: "Fife had heard. . . ." Reported by Mark Turner in "Sanctuary trial pits federal law vs. church duty," *Arizona Daily Star*, October 20, 1985.

Speak Truth to Power

Most of the courtroom events depicted in this section were witnessed by the author in her capacity as a reporter for the *Christian Science Monitor* and the Religious News Service. Quotes of testimony were verified with a copy of the certified trial transcripts at the law offices of Butler & Stein in Tucson.

The account of the trial given in this book is a vastly condensed version of what happened. Quotes, particularly those of the judge and lawyers, were shortened, and in a few cases, edited for clarity. Because examination of witnesses frequently took place over several days, the dates given are approximate.

17. Pages 92–93: Sources on the scene at Corbett's and Fife's houses on the morning of January 14, 1985, were the author's interviews with Jim Corbett, Tucson, November 1986, and with John Fife, Tucson, June 1986. Fife quoted his statement to Corbett in that interview. "Charges no surprise for movement leader," by Mark Turner, *Arizona Daily Star*, January 15, 1985, described the scene at Corbett's later that morning.

Page 92: Juana Beatriz Alvarez is a pseudonym.

Pages 93–95: Sources on the news conference in Phoenix, not attended by the author, were "Clergy among 16 indicted in alien 'railroad,'" by Chuck Hawley, Andy Hall, and Gene Varn, *Arizona Republic*, January 15, 1985, and "Law, morality likely to clash in alien-smuggling case," by Chuck Hawley, *Arizona Republic*, January 16, 1985. Reno's quotes appeared in the latter article.

Pages 95 (bottom)–96: Jim Corbett to author, Tucson, November 1985. John and Marianne Fife's remarks made in separate interviews with author, Tucson, July 1986.

Page 96: Page 27 of *Sanctuary*, edited by MacEoin, and pages 77–78 of *Sanctuary: The New Underground Railroad*.

Pages 96–97: Complete texts of the speeches made at the symposium are contained in *Sanctuary*, edited by MacEoin. Rev. William Sloane Coffin's quote is on page 138; Corbett's speech is on pages 183–197.

Pages 97–98: Sources on Jack Elder's and Stacey Merkt's trials were "Shelter chief is acquitted in alien case," by Dick Stanley, *Austin American-Statesman*, January 25, 1985, in which Steve Cooper was quoted; Bau, *This Ground Is Holy*, pages 81–83; "Sanctuary workers given prison terms," in the March 28, 1985, *Austin American-Statesman*, and a certified transcript of Merkt's and Elder's March 27, 1985, sentencing hearing, provided by the Neighborhood Justice Center, St. Paul, Minnesota.

Page 98, paragraph 2: *Sanctuary*, edited by MacEoin, pages 27–28, and "Reform Judaism assembly backs sanctuary movement," an AP story reported in the *Arizona Daily Star*, November 6, 1985.

Page 99, paragraph 1: Fife's comment was made to author, Tucson, June 1986. A portion of Elliott Abrams's Senate testimony on April 22, 1985, was reprinted in the July/August 1985 issue of *Common Cause*. Alan Nelson's quote was in Claudia Dreifus's February 1987 *Atlantic* article.

Page 99, paragraphs 2 and 3: MacEoin, *No Promised Land*, page 58, and "Second Class Refugees," by Arthur C. Helton, *New York Times*, April 2, 1985. Elliott Abrams's quote was in his January 17, 1985, editorial in the *Los Angeles Times*, "U.S. refugee policy is nothing to flee."

Pages 100 (bottom)–101: Republican Senator was quoted by Ed Baxter, aide to Senator Dennis DeConcini, in telephone interview from Washington, D.C., with the author, February 1987. Dreifus also reported this incident in the February 1987 *Atlantic*.

Page 101, paragraph 2: "Defendant, INS officer break bread together over asylum process," by Mark Turner, *Arizona Daily Star*, May 28, 1985.

Page 101, paragraph 3: "Retrial ordered in alien case," AP, as reported in the June 19, 1985, *New York Times*, and author's interview with Corbett, Tucson, July 1985.

Page 102, paragraph 2: "Sanctuary loses shield of religion," by Howard Fischer, *Arizona Daily Star*, July 26, 1985, and "Sanctuary trial pits federal law vs. church duty," by Mark Turner, *Arizona Daily Star*, October 20, 1985.

Page 102, paragraph 3: "Salvadoran refugee keeps punching in battle for asylum," by Guillermo X. Garcia, *Austin American-Statesman*, April 1986, special section; and Corbett, in *Sanctuary*, edited by MacEoin, page 194.

18. Page 104: "Sanctuary worker pleads guilty to lesser charge," by Howard Fischer, *Arizona Daily Star*, October 19, 1985, and "Sanctuary defendants say U.S. wants plea deal or prison terms," by Mark Turner, *Arizona Daily Star*, October 9, 1985. Corbett's statement made to author, Tucson, November 1985.

Page 105: Hirsh's comments were made in a February 1987 interview with author in Tucson.

Page 107: "Most said later...." See "Law Or Justice?" by Mitchell Pacelle, *The American Lawyer*, September 1986.

19. Page 108: Sources on Judge Carroll's evidentiary rulings include copies of Carroll's orders filed on October 25 and 28, 1985, in U.S. District Court in Tucson, as well as "Defense dealt another loss in sanctuary case," by Mark Turner, *Arizona Daily Star*, October 26, 1985, and "Last major defense barred in sanctuary case," by Mark Turner, *Arizona Daily Star*, October 29, 1985.

Page 108, paragraph 2: Corbett to author, Tucson, November 1986.

Pages 109–10: Fife was quoted in "Last major defense barred in sanctuary case," by Mark Turner, *Arizona Daily Star*, October 29, 1985. Thomas Chandler's remarks were made in telephone interview with author, Tucson, February 1987. Additional information on Judge Carroll's background was in "Carroll knows his job, peers say," by Mark Turner, *Arizona Daily Star*,

October 31, 1985. Hirsh's remarks were made in a February 1987 interview with the author in Tucson.

Pages 110–111: Martin's memo was quoted in "Agent urged caution in taking on 'Frito Bandito' railroad," by Carol Ann Bassett and Sandy Tolan, *Arizona Republic*, June 30, 1985. Thatcher's and Rayburn's memos were included with defense briefs filed with the court.

Pages 112–113: CIA, FBI, and NSC interest in sanctuary was reported in "Surveillance of Administration Critics," by Vicki Kemper, *Sojourners*, May 1987. Frank Varelli's February 1987 affidavit was included in a brief filed in federal court by James Brosnahan and Karen Snell on May 19, 1987, titled "Supplemental evidence in support of renewal of motion to dismiss for selective prosecution and impermissible political interference." A copy of this brief was provided to the author by A. Bates Butler, III.

Information on break-ins was contained in "Burglars or snoopers?" by Laurie Becklund, *Los Angeles Times*, January 30, 1986, and in "FBI inquiry sought in burglaries at sanctuary centers," by Carmen Duarte, *Arizona Daily Star*, January 31, 1986. Floyd Clarke was quoted in "FBI denies church-office break-ins," by Christopher Drew, *Chicago Tribune*, April 2, 1987.

20. Pages 114–115: Judge Carroll was quoted in "Judge warns sanctuary defense lawyers," by Mark Turner, *Arizona Daily Star*, November 20, 1985. Hirsh's comments were made in interview with author, Tucson, February 1987. Jurors were quoted by Mitchell Pacelle in *The American Lawyer*, September 1986.

21. Page 115: Sources on Salomón Graham include "Informers in the Sanctuary Movement," by Carol Ann Bassett and Sandy Tolan, *The Nation*, July 20–27, 1985, and "Informer removed as key witness in sanctuary case," by Gene Varn, *Arizona Republic*, October 4, 1985.

Page 117: Jurors were quoted by Mitchell Pacelle, *The American Lawyer*, September 1986.

22. Pages 118–121: Corbett's translation of Juana Alvarez's story, recorded in Mexico City in July 1984, was part of the *Sacramento Bee* series "Escape from El Salvador," August 1984.

Page 119: Father Paco is a pseudonym.

Page 121, paragraph 5: Carroll's quote was in a June 30, 1986, order reiterating his rejection of the international law and necessity defenses.

Page 122, paragraph 2: Corbett to author, Tucson, November 1986.

23. Page 122: Alejandro Rodríguez is a pseudonym.

Page 125: Rodríguez's second arrest by the INS was reported in "Rochester, N.Y., declares itself sanctuary city after witness's arrest," by

Daniel Browning, *Arizona Daily Star*, May 28, 1986. Rodríguez's departure to Canada was confirmed by Marilyn Mould of the Rochester Sanctuary Committee, in telephone interview with author, from Rochester, August 1987.

24. Page 125, bottom: Juror's remark was in *The American Lawyer*, September 1986.

Page 127: Miriam Hernández is a pseudonym. Corbett's comment was made to author, Tucson, February 1986. Joel Morelos and Francisco Nieto-Núñez are pseudonyms. The Nieto-Núñezes' story was told to the author by defense lawyers and by Jim Corbett.

Page 128, paragraph 3: Hirsh's and Corbett's comments made to author, Tucson, in February 1987, and November 1986.

25. Pages 128–131: Sources on the "Naco Five" incident were the author's interviews with Corbett, February and November 1986, and with Barry Lazarus and Cliff Pine, November 1986, in Tucson.

Page 129: ORDEN was referred to as the "eyes" and "fingers" of the National Guard on page 77 of *Salvador Witness*.

Pages 129–130: Quotes by border patrolmen and description of the Naco Border Patrol station, not visited by the author, were provided by Lazarus.

Pages 130 (bottom)–131: Corbett to author, Tucson, February 1986.

Page 131, paragraph 2: "U.S. won't prosecute 5 detained with Salvadorans," *Arizona Daily Star*, February 6, 1986, and author's conversations with Jim Corbett and Barry Lazarus, Tucson, February 5, 1986.

Pages 131–132: Corbett to author, Tucson, November 1986.

Page 132, paragraphs 3–4: Sister Nicgorski to author, Tucson, February 1986. The reference to "*contras* and ORDEN members" was in a December 3, 1983, letter from the Chicago Religious Task Force to Jim Corbett, Phil Conger, and John Fife. The January 1985 *Basta!*, pages II and VII, and *Sanctuary: The New Underground Railroad*, page 174, contained the other Chicago task force quotes on this page.

Pages 133–134: Corbett's statement of faith is in "A View From The Border," *Borders and Crossings*, pages 112–117.

26. Page 136: Juror quoted in *The American Lawyer*, September 1986.

27. Page 137: Elba Teresa Lopez is a pseudonym.

Page 138: Details of the break-in at the First United Methodist Church in Germantown, Pennsylvania, and the torture and murder of Joel Morelos's relatives in Guatemala were in a June 24, 1985, letter from attorneys Ellen Yaroshefsky and Michael Piccarreta to prosecutor Donald Reno. *No Prom-*

ised Land, page 38, and Jim Corbett were sources on the "Commandante Norma" incident.

Page 138: Pilar is a pseudonym.

Page 139: Dietrich quoted in "Escape from El Salvador," *Sacramento Bee*, August 26–30, 1984. Bill Johnston quoted in phone conversation with author, Tucson, July 1987. Fife quoted in interview with author, Tucson, June 1986.

Page 139, bottom: "Asylum denied Salvadoran who refused to testify in Tucson," an AP story as reported in the September 13, 1987, *Arizona Daily Star*.

28. Page 140: New York–based writer Julia Lieblich viewed a videotape of the raid on Sister Nicgorski's apartment and told the author about the "terrorism" file.

Page 141, paragraph 2: "Sanctuary defendants may get another day in court," by Daniel Browning, *Arizona Daily Star*, May 3, 1986.

Page 141, paragraph 3: Corbett to author, Tucson, July 1985. Haig's and Kirkpatrick's remarks were on pages 279 and 281 of *Salvador Witness*.

Page 142: Copies of pages from the FBI Terrorist Photo Album were included in defense briefs filed on May 19, 1987.

29. Page 143: Comments by Piccarreta and Butler were made to author, at press conference on March 14, 1986. Source for the cost of the trial was "Sanctuary case cost about $2.26 million," by Daniel Browning, *Arizona Daily Star*, June 1, 1986.

Pages 142 and 143: Jurors quoted in "Law Or Justice?" by Mitchell Pacelle, *The American Lawyer*, September 1986.

Page 144: Fife was quoted in "Defendants vow to resume work with movement," by Carmen Duarte and Jane Erikson, *Arizona Daily Star*, May 2, 1986. Corbett's quotes made to author, Tucson, November 1986. Father Quiñones's statement at the press conference was translated by Jesús Romo, assistant to attorney William Risner.

Page 146: Hirsh and Pat Corbett to author, Tucson, February and July 1987.

30. Page 147: Quiñones and Aguilar were quoted in "Two defendants denounce Carroll for banning 'Brown Virgin' parable," by Daniel Browning, *Arizona Daily Star*, April 12, 1986.

Page 148: Hirsh to author, Tucson, February 1987.

31. Page 148: Marianne Fife quoted herself to author, Tucson, July 1986.

Page 150: Corbett to author, Tucson, November 1986, and *Obedience to Authority: An Experimental View*, by Stanley Milgram, (Harper & Row, New York, 1974).

Page 151: Description of meeting and Peggy Hutchison's quote attributed by Marianne Fife, Tucson, July 1986. Reno's "pelted" quote in "Reno pleased that American justice system works," by Daniel Browning, *Arizona Daily Star*, May 2, 1986. Reno's statements at press conference attended by author, Tucson, May 1, 1986. Alan Nelson was quoted in "Politicians, legal experts draw their own conclusions about the trial," by Pam Izakowitz and Chris Limberis, *Arizona Daily Star*, May 2, 1986. Hirsh's remark at press conference attended by author, May 1, 1986.

Page 152: Cooper's comments made in telephone interview with author from St. Paul, Minnesota, June 1987. Corbett's quotes said to author, Tucson, November 1986.

Paragraph 2: Sheaffer quoted by Mark Shaffer and Dee Ralles in "Juror is at peace with verdicts, but other 'feels bad, really bad'," *Arizona Republic*, May 3, 1986.

Paragraphs 3–5: Jurors quoted in *Arizona Daily Star*, "Emotions of trial dogged diligent jury," by Jackie Rothenberg and Jim Erickson, May 2, 1986, and in Shaffer and Ralles's article in the May 3, 1986, *Arizona Republic*. "Law or Justice?" by Mitchell Pacelle, *The American Lawyer*, September 1986, was the source of quotes and descriptions of the jury deliberations.

Paragraph 6: Corbett to author, Tucson, November 1986.

32. Page 153: Author's interviews with Corbett, Klondyke, Arizona, August 1986, and Tucson, November 1986.

Page 154, paragraph 2: Fife was quoting Corbett here; see page 192 of *Sanctuary*, edited by MacEoin.

Page 155: Quiñones's remarks translated by court interpreter.

Page 156: Fife's comment to author, Tucson, February 1987. Chandler's remarks made in telephone interview with author, Tucson, February 1987.

Paragraph 5: Hirsh to author, Tucson, February 1987.

Paragraph 6: Reno quoted in "5 sanctuary defendants receive suspended sentences, probation," by Mark Turner and Daniel Browning, *Arizona Daily Star*, July 2, 1986.

Pages 157–158: Corbett to author, Tucson, November 1986.

Way Will Open

Page 159: Cerezo quote, translated by the author, was in "Central America: dueña de su destino," by Leyla Cattan, *Arizona Daily Star*, August 14, 1987.

Pages 159–160: The Mexican leftists incident was on page 16 of "Some Sanctuary Forms and Functions," by Corbett, a discussion draft dated June 5, 1987.

Page 160, paragraph 2: Reno's quote (*Seattle Times*, June 9, 1987), and other information in this paragraph from the "Annual report on Trsg sanctuary services," July 4, 1987.

Paragraph 3: Fife, telephone interview with author, Tucson, June 1987, and "U.S. sanctuary movement hopes to spread idea to Western Europe," by Mark Turner, *Arizona Daily Star*, September 18, 1986.

Pages 161–162: Dorothy Norvell Anderson, in the March 1987, Pima Monthly Meeting newsletter.

Page 162: "El Salvador expels 21 religious workers," UPI, as reported in the June 27, 1987, *Boston Globe*; "Salvadoran death squads may be in U.S.," by Paul Nussbaum of Knight-Ridder Newspapers, as reported in the July 14, 1987, *Arizona Daily Star*; "L.A. mayor vows to stem attacks on C. Americans," AP, as reported in the July 24, 1987, *Arizona Daily Star*; and "Moakley seeks investigation of INS official," by Ross Gelbspan, *Boston Globe*, August 6, 1987.

Pages 162 (bottom)–163: "Some Sanctuary Forms and Functions," pages 16–17 and 25.

Page 163, paragraph 2: Chandler to author, February 1987.

Page 164: Corbett, "Some Sanctuary Forms and Functions," page 12.

ACKNOWLEDGMENTS

I am deeply indebted to all the people who allowed me to interview them for this book, especially Jim Corbett, for their time and patience. I would also like to thank my family and friends, and in particular:

My editor, Greg McNamee, and writer David Quammen for their careful attention to the improvement of the manuscript;

John Longenecker, for his research notes that proved invaluable in writing the first half of the book;

The law offices of Butler & Stein, especially legal secretary Jessica Solon, for giving me access to the transcripts of the trial;

And photographers Sterling Vinson and Ricardo Valdivieso, for their generous contribution of their work.

The following people were also of significant help to me:

Carol Ann Bassett, José Luis Pérez Canchola, Joe Crow, Guillermo Garcia, Arthur Keating, Julia Lieblich, Ray Lisansky, Jim McGovern, Chris Medvescek, Jim Salmons, John Stickler, Ann Russell, and Paul Weich.

I would especially like to thank my mother, Dr. Florence Davidson, for her support and encouragement.

INDEX

ABOUT THE AUTHOR

MIRIAM DAVIDSON grew up in the Boston, Massachusetts, area and became a Quaker when she was 11 years old. After graduating with a degree in English from Yale University in 1982, she moved to South Texas, where she worked as a volunteer for the American Friends Service Committee and as a reporter and Lifestyle editor for the *Laredo News*. She subsequently served as managing editor of *Third Coast* magazine in Austin, Texas. Her interest in the sanctuary movement led her to Tucson, Arizona, in 1985, where she covered the trial of the eleven sanctuary workers for the *Christian Science Monitor* and the Religious News Service. She resides in Tucson and regularly attends Pima Friends Meeting.